REVIVING READING

2/07/07

To Michael —
Thanks for
your inspiration &
motivation - you
make it all
doable!

Alison

REVIVING READING

School Library Programming, Author Visits and Books that Rock!

Alison M. G. Follos

Foreword by Jack Gantos

LIBRARIES
UNLIMITED
A Member of the Greenwood Publishing Group
Westport, Connecticut • London

Library of Congress Cataloging-in-Publication Data

Follos, Alison M. G.
  Reviving reading: school library programming, author visits, and books that rock! / by Alison M.G. Follos; foreword by Jack Gantos.
      p. cm.
  Includes bibliographical references and index.
  ISBN 1-59158-356-X (pbk: alk. paper)
  1. Middle school libraries—Activity programs—United States.   2. Reading promotion—United States.   3. Teenagers—Books and reading—United States.
  4. Preteens—Books and reading—United States.   5. School librarian participation in curriculum planning—United States.   6. Young adult literature—Study and teaching (Middle school)   7. Young adult literature—Bibliography.   I. Title.
  Z675.S3F555 2006
  028.5'5—dc22   2006017616

British Library Cataloguing in Publication Data is available.

Library of Congress Catalog Card Number: 2006017616
ISBN: 1-59158-356-X

First published in 2006

Libraries Unlimited, 88 Post Road West, Westport, CT 06881
A Member of the Greenwood Publishing Group, Inc.
www.lu.com

Printed in the United States of America

The paper used in this book complies with the Permanent Paper Standard issued by the National Information Standards Organization (Z39.48–1984).

10 9 8 7 6 5 4 3 2 1

Dedicated to my mother, Stevie Capozio, who taught me to nourish the dream, and my father, M. R. Dubin (April 16, 1916–January 14, 1997), who told me, "Always keep your sense of humor."

CONTENTS

FOREWORD

After reading the introduction to Alison Follos's essential book on literacy and literature, you may feel—as a reader—that you are on the endangered species list. Perhaps you will imagine yourself as a carnival act in which a curtain is pulled aside by a cigar-smoking barker who has gathered a crowd to watch as you sit upon a stage in an easy chair, actually reading a book.

"Look, the *creature* is reading a book!" the barker exclaims.

The audience gasps. How arcane, they think. How primitive.

I know there are times when readers feel alienated from society and so disconnected from the non-reading majority that they feel the need to check into a mental hospital. This impulse seems reasonable, given that the staff will probably give them a nice room with a view, a comfortable chair, and a reading lamp. The risk is that they may never give up the reading habit and the staff will not release them.

But there is hope for those suffering from the affliction of reading: Instead of a hospital, one can just check into a library and check out with a fresh book. And in each book there may be something to read about that is so engrossing that time vanishes as the imagination replaces consciousness. Ahhh, what could be better than that? To sit in your own home—on the stage of your own life—and think to yourself, "Yes, this creature chooses to read."

Like you, I am one of these reading creatures. And as a result of so much reading, I decided to write books, too. I decided to do this when I was young, and I went to college for writing. I published my first book for children (*Rotten Ralph*) in 1976 and, shortly after, the publisher asked me to visit a school or two and read to kids. That sounded grand. But the reality was less so. I was a bit green at commanding the attention of young students, and the schools were uneven with regard to preparing for me, and how to follow up after I was gone.

Fortunately I've grown up some and refined my creative writing and literature visits, and the schools have become far savvier at preparation and integrating the literature and creative writing into the curriculum. So for me—and for Alison Follos—there is great hope with regard to reading and all of the many benefits a life of the mind offers. Plus, at no time have more and better books for children been published. Also, the numbers of fine authors who are willing to visit schools are many. And we find that in the colleges that offer degrees in teaching that children's literature is stressed as an essential component of a solid education.

And, libraries are often the hub of the school life. In other words, the building blocks are in place for great success with literacy.

However, success will not happen without smarts and effort. Alison Follos animates these building blocks through her clear and practical approaches to elevating a school's zest for literature. Like any good book chock full of teaching tips, take ownership of it. Use what you can. Put it to work. Add what you will to your toolbox of teaching. We will always be a field of dedicated teachers. We will always have impressionable young minds to mentor, and we will be an unrelenting force for the pleasure of the imagination and the power of books to elevate our minds. We believe this so much we want to share it with others—and this book shares the experience of a master teacher and librarian. She is one of us.

Jack Gantos

ACKNOWLEDGMENTS

Thanks to my family for their patience while I was married to this project.

Thanks to Jody Kopple—teacher, librarian, and friend—for her careful and attentive reviewing.

Special thanks to Timothy Follos, for his smart, sure, and dedicated editorial assistance.

Finally, thanks to North Country School for the sabbatical leave and the faith.

INTRODUCTION: PROMOTING LITERATURE

I work at a small boarding farm school in the Adirondack Mountains of upstate New York. Our middle school students come from all over the world to a place that fosters childhood, hard work, environmental stewardship, and individuality within community. We're an adoptive, adaptive, and active place: lots of kid energy, fall harvests, animals to be cared for in the subzero winter, mountains to be climbed at every opportunity, dance, theater, arts, planting gardens, and tapping maple trees in the spring. Fitting traditional academics into the day is a challenge. Fitting in any additional programming is disruptive. And fitting reading into the mix is a Herculean effort. But isn't that the case in every household and classroom in our culture these days? We're a busy society, and it doesn't seem that we make time to read, or worse, consider it important. If reading is to be preserved within our culture, we must carve out more time for free-reading—not only in schools, but in every household in America. The other day one of my biggest readers came in to say, "Finally, I'm going to have some time to read. We're going on a three-day car trip." I thought, "How ironic. In a nation rich with leisure time and material goods, our reading time is impoverished."

NPR's book critic Maureen Corrigan writes in her recent book *Leave Me Alone, I'm Reading* (New York: Random House, 2005):

> But here's a catch: I live an intensely bookish life during a resolutely nonliterary era. An absurdly small number of people in America care about what I or any other book critic has to say about the latest novel or work of nonfiction. Despite the proliferation of mega-bookstores and neighborhood reading groups, most Americans are indifferent to the lure of literature: in fact, according to a *Wall Street Journal* article of a few years ago, some 59 percent of Americans don't own a single book. Not a cookbook or even the Bible...[1]

The 2002 National Endowment for the Arts (NEA) report was aptly titled "Reading at Risk: A Survey of Literary Reading in America." It states, "Indeed, at the current rate of loss, literary reading as a leisure activity will virtually disappear in half a century."[2] This report reaffirms a well-known fact: Reading for pleasure is a dwindling pastime in our culture.

Again, from the NEA report, "As more Americans lose this capability, our nation becomes less informed, active, and independent-minded. These are not qualities that a free, innovative, or productive society can afford to lose."[3]

What does this mean? To me it means I must work harder to promote what I believe is important. I believe that reading is important as a leisure activity, as a recreational activity, as an intellectual endeavor. English and reading specialists teach children how to read. Librarians can show students *why* they would ever *want* to read. We can give our students stories that they'll get pleasure from, that will embolden their lives, and above all else, that will prove that reading is worth the effort. This book is about introducing reading in a manner that is appealing to kids and will have it become a natural part of their lifelong habits.

The following chapters offer a compilation of programs that promote reading throughout the school. Many of the programs are ready and set-to-go: Simply follow the guidelines and put them in place in your own school. Others are easily adaptable to suit the special needs of your school. Some, like our whole-school reading incentive program (see Title Trekking, Chapter 7), use a symbolic theme, matching books to the geographical landscape (mountains, in our case), and they can be creatively customized to match popular landmarks within your own community—lakes, rivers, avenues, animals, or even popular kid interests such as movie stars, rock musicians, snowboard companies, etc. Here are immediate solutions to put in place to combat the hand wringing and inaction brought on by the panic over raising a nation of nonreaders.

There's no magic. These programs took me seventeen years to fine-tune. You won't implement all of them overnight. Having said that, don't be discouraged. Big ideas develop in little stages. If you want to shift the frenetic pace in your school, take slow and steady action. That's the difference between developing long-term programming and flash-in-the-pan trends.

I struggle with numbers. In my number-snarled mind, budgets are made to be stretched. When I know that something is going to be good for the library, I want it. To ward off budget limitations, I fundraise and apply for grants. In the following chapters you'll find that grant writing really isn't hard—time consuming, yes, but the extra cash is worth the effort. Book fairs help provide fun books, author visits, and other special additions to the school library. The extra programming that fundraising produces helps to eradicate the misnomer of *boring* from reading.

Hosting an author visit can transform the mysterious impact of stories into the extraordinary chapters of everyday life. Offering students the opportunity to talk with an author about who they are and how writing has affected their lives—and especially how their lives have affected their writing—is an exchange that guarantees interest. The voice behind the work endorses and validates everything you know is true about the power of literature, and more important, convinces your students. Author visits are so valuable that you'll begin to think about how to host more than one a year.

Don't let a skimpy budget thwart a good idea that connects kids with books. Go for creative funding. You will note that Jack Gantos and Tim Wynne-Jones are mentioned frequently within this book. They are each authors who have the unusual ability to connect with K–12 schools. If you are able to afford only one author a year, this whole-school connection is a must. These authors have written children's picture books, middle school titles, short stories, young adult fiction, and adult novels. Their literature is carefully crafted and will survive the test of time. They have changed the way I am able to teach because of their respect for the reader, their commitment to literature, and quite simply, their profound literary talents. They write the antithesis of dumbed-down literature and create stories that become increasingly meaningful with each reading.

Today's potential young readers are picky and busy. The competition for their attention is fierce. To catch their eyes, literature should be short, funny, scary, and, above all else, highly *readable* if a writer-reader partnership is to happen. The right stuff isn't worth a hoot if we can't get students to take a look. That's why reading incentive programs and literature appreciation classes are imperative. You'll learn how to implement these into the busiest curriculums and communities.

Keep your library a place that feels good to be in. I try to steer away from an overly institutional environment. Cushy chairs, pillows, and decorative and soothing colors help create an atmosphere that supports calm, contemplation, and concentration. From the beginning I tell students that every library in the whole wide world speaks a universal language: the quiet language. We talk about the luxury of sharing a common space with friends and teachers while maintaining the right to have our own uninterrupted thoughts. I know that kids are kids. They need to be active. There are quiet activities that students may do while listening to a story, or while surrounded by other folks who are reading, writing or studying. They can knit, draw, or make origami figures, but they need to do it quietly. The library is a great place to "model" reading—having quietly active children among quietly active readers is a good beginning.

Knowing what titles will best suit your audience demands constant attention. The following pages will give you some ideas on how to keep up with hot titles, intellectual gems, and sweeping trends—including what you might scoff at as "literature". If you're going to lead the way, you must blaze the trail. This means staying nonjudgmental, flexible, and open-minded—tough stuff for professionals taught to make order out of chaos. Michael Sullivan, a proponent of using different strategies to break down the barriers that boys have to reading, has written, "Since some boys may not read more than one book a year, we certainly don't want them 'wasting' their time on *Captain Underpants*. But this is faulty reasoning. We need to realize that if boys read something that speaks to them, they are much more likely to read other books."[4]

Jon Scieszka, a children's master of nonsense, writes, "Why is tragedy seen as being more substantial than comedy? Why do we believe sadness is a more valid and a deeper emotion than happiness? Why is it that funny stuff never wins the awards? (What was the last funny movie to win an Academy Award: Or, closer to home, in our world of children's books—what was the last funny book to win a Newbery?)"[5] Children love humor, and we ignore this. Any wonder that they ignore our recommendations? In other words, don't cast personal aspersions on what children are reading if it doesn't suit your standards. Let them read what they like and they'll like to read. Strong reading comprehension, vocabulary, and spelling are more likely to develop when children read a lot, as opposed to their suffering a couple of titles that an adult has forced upon them.

SUPPORT FROM THE TEAM

For kids to be convinced that children's and young adult (YA) literature matters, parents and educators need to believe it too. A paradox in education is that adults preach that children should read yet seldom take the time to read children's books. To counter this oddity, begin a reading incentive program for your faculty. Designing a whole-school reading program reinforces the merits of reading through visibility. When adults are introduced to children's and YA titles, they discover how wonderful these stories are and you'll have a hard time keeping these new converts in books. Faculty who are aware of these titles spread the word, and their enthusiasm is infectious. Booktalks are an advertisement about a book, a quickly delivered verbal blurb designed to nab interest. Booktalks from the coolest adults in the middle school will fuel the popularity of catchy titles, and students will be after their teachers to return the hot picks. It's a win-win situation. Students who see adults reading children's and YA titles value the integrity of the material.

I believe that the value of literature in our students' lives is so important that we must do more than dictate, assign, and worry about it. We must become part of the solution. We must provide time and a quiet environment to allow students the pleasurable luxury to read. Doing so means either eking time out from another activity or folding reading into the established academic schedule. Reclaiming readers will rejuvenate the spirit of a society that's run ragged, stressed-out, overconnected, intellectually complacent, and emotionally dissatisfied.

Reading requires discipline, as do most intellectual and athletic pursuits. *Discipline*, as in: to train by teaching or instruction; to develop by instruction and exercise; to train in self-control or obedience to standards. To the athlete, such demands are expected and accepted, but for today's students, literacy is difficult to attain. There is just so much new stuff for them to do and only the same old amount of time in which to do it. Simply put, reading is getting crammed-out of the scene. So it comes down to this: If reading is a democratic free right, then reviving reading is worth our fight.

NOTES

1. Maureen Corrigan, *Leave Me Alone, I'm Reading: Finding and Losing Myself in Books* (New York: Random House, 2005).

2. Conclusion to "Reading at Risk: A Survey of Literary Reading in America," National Endowment for the Arts, 2002 report, p. xiii.

3. Dana Gioia, preface to "Reading at Risk: A Survey of Literary Reading in America," National Endowment for the Arts, 2002 report.

4. Michael Sullivan, "Why Johnny Won't Read," *School Library Journal*, Aug. 2004, pp. 36–39.

5. Jon Sceiszka, "What's So Funny, Mr. Scieszka?" *Horn Book Magazine*, Nov./Dec. 2005, p. 655.

Part I

WHY LITERATURE

Chapter 1

WHY LITERATURE IS IMPORTANT NOW

To anyone that believes in the importance of reading, the 2002 National Endowment for the Arts (NEA) report was bleak. Entitled "Reading at Risk: A Survey of Literary Reading in America," it is a massive compilation of comprehensive stats and figures. The impressive report reaffirms one fact: Reading for pleasure is a dwindling pastime in our culture. Past NEA Chairman Dana Gioia states, "The important thing now is to understand that America can no longer take active and engaged literacy for granted."[1]

School librarians were not surprised by the evidence. Over the past twenty years, young adults (18–24 age group) have gone from being those most likely to read to those least likely. Their documented decline was 55 percent greater than that of the total adult population.[2]

Stephen Krashen, in his well-received book *The Power of Reading* writes, "There is no literacy crisis, at least not the kind of crisis the media have portrayed. There are, first of all, very few people who have been through the educational system who are completely unable to read and write. In fact, literacy, defined simply as the ability to read and write on a basic level, has been steadily rising in the United States for the last hundred years."

Krashen continues, "There is, however, a problem. Nearly everyone in the United States can read and write. They just don't read and write well enough. Although basic literacy has been on the increase for the last century, the demands for literacy have been rising faster. Many people clearly don't read and write well enough to handle the complex literacy demands of modern society. The problem is thus not how to bring students to the second- or third-grade reading level; the problem is how to bring them beyond this."[3]

Parents and educators commiserate over why kids won't read and lament over their obsessive consumption of electronic media. They complain about the amount of TV children watch, they fret over the aggressive video games kids play, they bemoan the number of consecutive hours teens spend "I.M.-ing" (instant messaging) each other, and on and on. Yet adults are equally caught up in the maddening futility of keeping pace in a tech-savvy world. Through an increasing wave of electronic preoccupation, literary reading as a reflective and intellectual process that demands attention span and concentration is falling by the wayside.

The bottomline questions are: How important is literature anymore? Can we live without it? Our children seem to be doing so, but at what cost? At what loss?

These are questions with which we must reckon as we witness the downward trend of reading scores and the deviant social trends of teen sex, violence, depression, suicide, homelessness, runaways, and substance abuse. Literature can introduce thoughts that differ from those of a student's peers, teachers, and families; in short, it can pierce the status quo of their lives. It can unsettle and disturb their complacent indifference. Reading isn't the single answer, but it raises consciousness. It encourages students to think for themselves. Through the liberating experience of independent reading, students are entitled to the hard-won treasure that our forefathers fought for: intellectual freedom.

With the fate of reading at risk, proactive measures will ensure that literature has a place in our children's busy lives. The overarching purpose of intentional reading programs is to make a fuss and substantiate the rewards of immersing literature throughout the curriculum. If we show our children how to derive pleasure from the cooperative and independent acts of reading, we contribute toward their cognitive and intellectual growth.

Jennifer Donnelly (*A Northern Light*, San Diego, CA: Harcourt, 2003), in her closing speech at the New York Library Association's Youth Services conference (April 2005), said:

> Someone once commented on my use of war terminology in talking about books and reading—my use of words like *fighting* and *front lines*. I use these words because I truly believe that this is a battle. It is nothing less than a fight against mediocrity and mindlessness. Against bad media and thoughtless consumerism. Against ignorance and hopelessness, cynicism and despair. Getting our children—all of our children—to read is one of the most critical battles that modern society faces. Why?
>
> Because here in America, the most powerful country in the world, nearly 13 million children live in poverty. And this number is rising. Here, the average child watches four hours of television a day—even though studies tell us that too much television increases the risk of aggressive behavior, attention deficit disorder, obesity and substance abuse. And here, many children can recognize Ronald McDonald and Mickey Mouse, but have a little more trouble with Abraham Lincoln, Susan B. Anthony, or Martin Luther King, Jr.[4]

REALITY READING

As parents and educators, if we introduce novels that speak to teens about the things that are of interest to them, we offer perspective within their own vantage point. Edgy subject matter may feel like it's sending a confused or daring message, but the content is out there. The scariest fiction allows teens a vicarious experience, from a safe place.

The effects that stories have on people need little endorsement. From the oral traditions of antiquity to the trendy graphic novels of today, getting lost in a story is an inexplicable pleasure. Yet it's a dying pleasure that needs reintroduction. In nearly every school library there is the student that visits daily and finds everything they love to read. Then there is everybody else. We need to court everybody else.

Children and teens are allowed less and less time for this edifying form of recreation. Their time is scheduled full of after-school activities or gobbled up by incessant electronic connections. Even teens that like to read can barely find a conducive or protected time to do so. The less time and opportunity provided for student free-reading, the more accepting, and thus complacent, we all become about not reading. And for students who've never felt the inclination to read, reading becomes increasingly foreign and heavy with misgivings. Recently, a parent resignedly noted to me his son's reading interest, remarking, "Unless it comes across his video screen or cell phone text-messaging, he's not going to read it."

Before the Adirondack Northway was constructed, our family traveled from Connecticut to New York's Adirondack Mountains via old State Route 9N, a seemingly endless winding road that connected rural towns with odd names. I lay in the back of the station wagon stocked with pillows, books, magazines, and *Archie* and *Casper* comic books. Captured in a moving cocoon, I sank into a reading reverie for six hours. Today, before beginning a long trip, parents plug movies into their vehicle's video player. Reading has become old-fashioned and low on the totem pole of a free-choice leisure activity. It's easily overshadowed by easy-access screen animation. As Gioia notes, "Reading itself is a progressive skill that depends on years of education and practice. By contrast, most electronic media such as television, recordings, and radio make fewer demands on their audiences, and indeed often require no more than passive participation. Even interactive electronic media, such as video games and the Internet, foster shorter attention spans and accelerated gratification."[5]

CONVINCING STUDENTS THAT READING ISN'T BORING

The amount of single focus and concentration that reading requires seems disproportionate in our multitasked society. To expect kids to focus all their attention upon black scrawls on an inanimate page is a challenge. It's hard for them. Literature doesn't visually offer color or images like a TV show. It doesn't offer sound. It won't overtly entertain them. Readers must make the first overture before a story will unfold. Readers envision the story. Like repeatedly flexing and strengthening muscle, the repeated concentration that reading demands strengthens concentration, verbal skills, and higher-level thinking. It proposes differing perspectives and stimulates ideas. It invigorates coagulated mental stamina. What exercise does for the heart, reading does for the brain.

The National Institute for Literacy reported that:

a smaller percentage of 13- and 17-year-olds read for fun daily in 1999 than in 1984;

a smaller percentage of 17-year-olds saw adults reading in their homes in 1999 than in 1984; and

a greater percentage of 17-year-olds were watching three or more hours of television each day in 1999 than in 1978[6]

In the 2004 results from the National Assessment of Educational Progress (NAEP), Chester Finn Jr., president of the Thomas B. Fordham Foundation, a conservative think tank, said the lack of reading improvement on the NAEP tests is cause for "what ought to be pretty deep alarm."[7] Only three states progressed at even the lower, "basic," level according to the report.

To make matters worse, research shows that boys are becoming endangered readers. Michael Sullivan, *Connecting Boys with Books*,[8] spoke at a professional development conference at North Country School in 2005. He candidly addressed boys and their reading problems. According to Sullivan's research, boys enter school reading a year and a half behind girls. By the time they reach the 11th grade, boys are reading three years behind girls. In a recent study of high school sophomores, boys said—if they admitted to reading at all—they read about 2.3 hours a week; girls admitted to reading an average of 2.6 hours a week. Michael said, "We're closing the gap, but it's in the wrong direction."[9] Children in America don't feel that reading is important. Michael Sullivan pointed out two obvious truths: Men read in isolation—the bathroom for instance; women read in book groups. Thus, boys don't see men reading, and they lack role models. Perhaps, through this glaring absence, boys don't feel reading has any relevance in their lives.

Mike ran these statistics by us: In school, boys fail at twice the rate as girls; 80 percent of high school dropouts are male; 90 to 95 percent of kids coded with ADHD (attention-deficit hyperactivity disorder) are male; 75 percent of remedial classes are male and 1 in 3 boys are in remedial reading classes by the time they're in 3rd grade. There are a variety of theories on why this is so, but there is one obvious reality: Boys and girls *are* different. They develop differently and they learn differently. At age 11½, a girl has a fully developed adult brain; a boy's brain reaches that same development at age 14½. So here's the catch: When educators decided it was time to do something about girls' learning problems in math and science, did they pump girls with steroids to make them more assertive and build-up their confidence? No, we changed our teaching strategies and reassessed our instructional practices. As Michael Sullivan said, "School systems aren't going to fix the problem. Teachers will."[10]

The act of independent reading is physically passive. The positive effects are invisible to a child trying to witness and understand the attraction. Developing an interest in reading must be intentionally delivered. Introducing the recreational and entertainment value of story develops a taste for literature. Having a carefully designed class to foster the intellectual and emotional reactions that literature stirs uncovers the power of literature. Literature appreciation classes should be a part of every school's curriculum, and librarians should be part of the team to make this happen. We call our literature class Reader's Workshop (see Reader's Workshop, Chapter 8).

TODAY'S LITERATURE FOR TODAY'S KIDS

Interrupt-that-thought has become our modus operandi. We shuffle between real-time conversations, e-mail, cell phone, Googling, voice mail, headline news chopped-up by commercial messages, and so on. The average child lives in a household with 2.9 TVs, 1.8 VCRs, 3.1 radios, 2.1 CD players, 1.4 video game players, and 1 computer.[11] Students walking through the library door have an almost palpable attraction to the computer stations.

Inquiring minds are intoxicated by the allure of entering an electronic query and receiving an instantaneous, impersonal response. Written correspondence has shifted from carefully composed and newsy letter writing to quick, cursory, and diced-up e-mails. Nuances are misconstrued and miscommunication is rampant. I once had a visiting author comment, "I never knew if you loved me or hated me." He couldn't interpret my quickly jotted comments that I rushed off between classes. Our reading habits are following suit, skimming quick "hits" of information rather than pondering over longer, purposefully composed literary material. Reading and writing in our fast-dashed culture have become something of an anomaly. Students consider mastering language skills an old-fashioned discipline to be suffered. Reading demands time, attention, and concentration— all precious commodities. Creative measures need to be in place if we are to shift our students' reliance from quick-hit information to the gratification of reading for pleasure, relaxation, and enlightenment.

All the bright shiny covers in the children's section won't attract the disin-clined. We need an assertive approach. Motivating children to read begins with creating an introduction to and connection with stories. Taking action is never easy, especially when hampered by piles of work and imposed educational standards. It demands endless energy and confidence in the face of daily de-mands and doubts. The following chapters will show you some commonsense instructional strategies that are simple to integrate into the entire school. Know that you can do something, and that by implementing programming, one pro-gram at a time, you will save many students from being left behind. That's a great beginning.

NOTES

1. Dana Gioa, conclusion to "Reading at Risk: A Survey of Literary Reading in America," National Endowment for the Arts, 2002 report, p. xiii.

2. Ibid., p. xi.

3. Stephen D. Krashen, *The Power of Reading* (Westport, CT: Libraries Unlimited, 2004), pp. ix–x.

4. Jennifer Donnelly, "Bringing the Pieces Together," closing speech at the New York Library Association's NYLA Youth Services Section spring conference, April 1, 2005, Bolton Landing, NY.

5. "Reading at Risk," p. vii.

6. National Institute for Literacy's Online Reading Facts, NEA 2002, p. 39. Available at http://www.nifl.gov.

7. Robert Tomsho, "Reading Scores Advance Little in National Test," *Wall Street Journal* (Eastern Edition), Oct. 20, 2005, p. B.1.

8. Michael Sullivan, *Connecting Boys to Books* (Chicago: American Library Associa-tion, 2003).

9. Michael Sullivan, *Connecting Boys to Books* speech at North Country School Pro-fessional Development program, Nov. 10, 2005, Lake Placid, NY.

10. Ibid.

11. "Reading at Risk," p. xii.

Chapter 2

MASS-COMMUNICATION PILE-UP

Literature, like any art, is a give-and-take medium. Without personal interaction, a book is just another object collecting dust on the shelf. Written language, beginning with the cuneiform system developed by the Sumerians and hieroglyphs of ancient Egypt, originated to facilitate economic trade, convey cultural identity, and preserve traditions.

Today we have innumerable other ways to communicate and are not dependent on the written word for commerce. Yet written language, composed to communicate independent and original thoughts, is still the most reliable manner to document, and interpret, individual opinion. Quality literature affects our spirit, sparks our intellect, extends our interpersonal relationships, and explores the ordinary to expose the extraordinary. Literature connects centuries, transcends time, crosses borders, and above all, validates free choice. It communicates the individuality that defines us. It pushes past darting everyday anxieties—"Will my parents find out that I skipped school?" "When will I get the project finished?"—and absorbs readers into a deeper dimension of concentration.

Authors write books to be read. That single event, or series of events, activates the thought process. It requires concentration and effort. Caught within the grip of a good story, readers imagine a sequence of images that an author has created. Their involvement with the story spurs them to predict, suspect, and project what happens. If the reader fails to bring a single focused attention and intellectual engagement to the reading, the story fails to emerge. Young adult (YA) author Jennifer Donnelly adroitly comments, "Books demand participation. They make kids show up. They engage their heads and their hearts."[1]

Compounded and instigated by solitary contemplation, literature stirs up emotions. Without moving past the page it's a miracle of inner-cerebral travel to wonderlands of infinite potential. It's an affirmation that we aren't alone in our zaniness, our most spirited, magical, or misunderstood selves. It has the omnipotent facility of unfolding anywhere, the adaptive capacity to merge and release an unfathomable realm of notions within the most concrete and restricted confines. Through the unfolding of a story a prisoner is released.

In "Reading at Risk," past NEA report chairman Dana Gioia writes, "Reading is not a timeless, universal capability. Advanced literacy is a specific intellectual skill and social habit that depends on a great many educational, cultural, and economic factors. As more Americans lose this capability, our nation becomes less informed, active, and independent-minded. These are not qualities that a free, innovative, or productive society can afford to lose."[2]

Even closer to the heart of literary influence on the young, Jennifer Donnelly concludes:

> At the beginning of my talk . . . I said that I believe that getting children to read was a fight against things, against negative things like cynicism and despair. It's also a fight for something. It's a fight for knowledge and hope. For tolerance, compassion, and freedom. For beauty and wonder. Books can work magic. They can change lives. They can make children think and feel, when so much of the world conspires to numb young minds and emotions. Books can break boundaries—the ones inside of us and the ones outside of us. They can sweep away misperceptions and misconceptions, heal what is damaged, and unite us.[3]

IN AN AGE OF INFORMATION, WHY IS LITERATURE IMPORTANT?

Ancient oral storytelling served a multitude of community needs. It preserved and passed down cultural traditions, entertained, embellished the trophy tales from the tribal providers, and congregated a people to strengthen social, cultural, and political affiliation.

Native American traditional monster tales had several purposes, but first and foremost was that of keeping children safe. The scariest monster stories were told to the youngest children, intent on frightening them from exploring too far from the village, where a hungry predator or a raging river might claim their life. The real side of scary stories could be worse.

As parents and educators, if we introduce novels that speak to teens about the things that are of interest to them, we're providing perspective for their own interpretation. Edgy subject matter may feel like it's sending a confused or conflicting message, but the content is out there. The scariest fiction allows teens a vicarious experience, a forewarning from a safe zone, and anyone familiar with inner-city street life will attest that the real side of scary can be fatal. Having youth read "all about it" is preferable to living some of it.

Tim Wynne-Jones has written:

> Fiction abounds in this age of matterless data. It is the stuff of video games, the fluff of chatlines, at once candid and insincere and, finally, as ephemeral as the medium across which it flickers. Fiction, now as ever, serves merely to distract. For fiction is, after all, only a means of transport. Story offers more: the goods. Story is the freight that fiction, at its best, delivers. Story has shape, weight, and consequence. Story matters.[4]

A screen delivers messages so quickly viewers need only to show up and watch. They're taken on a visual ride of rapid-fire ideas that leaves no time for processing or consideration. Left to this diet, a young screen-fed viewer is easily manipulated and influenced. Before the viewer can get away, there's some new madcap show flagging their attention. This one-sided mode of communication is absent of personal connection or investment. At best it's fun for day-after social chitchat. At worse it spawns a zoned-out reaction. The increase in electronic connection seems in direct proportion to the withdrawn and isolated social patterns of our culture.

Story is absorbed at an individual's own pace. It must be interesting enough for the reader to invest time and attention to it. In a culture that prioritizes entertainment above substance, today's best literature entertains brilliantly and prompts introspection subtly. It offers material that students can use to measure up, compare, reconsider, reevaluate, and best of all, reflect and think about. Without the reader's commitment and investment in the story, it won't happen. The silent communication that unfolds in story carries the serene satisfaction of being able to be interrupted time and time again. A story will wait patiently, indefinitely, for a reader's renewed attention. Other than the family dog, where else can you establish that loyal devotion?

SUFFERING FROM READING DEPRIVATION

Reading, like any other discipline, requires practice for one to become proficient at it. All readers do not read equally. In general, little girls acquire language skills earlier than little boys do. Michael Sullivan, author of *Connecting Boys to Books*, refers to a 1998 survey of UCLA college freshmen, that when asked how many hours they spend reading for pleasure, 35 percent of the males and 22 percent of the females answered, "None."[5] That's a sorry testament from a country of well-educated students. It illuminates this paradox: Students are reading less as they progress through our educational system.

A March 2005 *USA Today* read, "The USA's children live in an increasingly heavy stew of media, spending about 6½ hours a day mostly watching TV, using computers and enjoying other electronic activities. And they are spending relatively little time reading or doing homework; a Kaiser Family Foundation survey reported."[6] In one year an avid 13-year-old TV consumer will have witnessed 7,000 screen murders. While skipping out on homework, youngsters are being *entertained* with violence.

Sven Birkerts writes:

> When I contemplate the substantial decline of literary reading, I can't help but envision a culture increasingly impoverished in its means of expression, lacking not just the verbal nuances, the appreciation of meanings and shades of meanings, but also the syntactical lexicon, the internalized sense of what structures best serve different needs in conversation as well as writing. Our thinking, our evaluation of the world—psychologically, morally—depends enormously on our ability to grasp and present concepts, and for this a developed sense of language is essential. A culture that has grown linguistically slack is susceptible to every sort of rhetoric and demagoguery.

Birkerts continues, "Frightening as this is to think about, the prospect of a large-scale loss of creative imagination, especially in the young, is more frightening still. For imagination is the seedbed of inwardness, of subjective depth. Reading quickens and enriches this faculty."[7]

Literature remains a free-choice leisure activity that has yet to be completely manipulated by mass marketing. Yes, there is the Harry Potter exception, but what Harry's done for reading is worth noting. Brilliant and excessive marketing has elevated his exposure, thus, his appeal. Recently, while surrounded by adult physical therapists, I listened as they lauded the latest exploits of the Potter tribe.

I was bemused by their enthusiastic rapture over the Potter phenomenon. One professional bragged, "I read all night and into the next morning. I missed work that day." From Harry they jumped into a conversation about Charlie (of Chocolate Factory fame), and how Gene Wilder was a much better Willy Wonka than Johnny Depp. What was going on? These physical therapists had no children, but they were keenly aware of some very popular children's titles.

If publishers had the same budgets as Hollywood or Microsoft, who can say how popular reading would become? Literature is an overlooked mode of entertainment for the young, and coincidentally, it lacks commercial backing. The youth in our country spend untold amounts of time, attention, and money on fashion, music, videos, and self-indulged entertainment—entertainment that's promoted by in-your-face advertising. When was the last time you noticed a hot YA title plugged on television? (The book, not the movie.) Except for mass-market titles, traditionally the children and YA sections in bookstores and public libraries are housed in low-profile areas. They seem to be deliberately tucked away.

NOTES

1. Jennifer Donnelly, closing speech at the NYLA/YSS spring conference, April 1, 2005.

2. Dana Gioia, preface to "Reading at Risk: A Survey of Literary Reading in America, Research Division Report #46, National Endowment for the Arts, 2002.

3. Jennifer Donnelly, closing speech at the NYLA/YSS spring conference, April 1, 2005.

4. Tim Wynne-Jones, "Short Tempered," *Horn Book Magazine*, May/June 1999, pp. 293–300.

5. Michael Sullivan, *Connecting Boys with Books* (Chicago: American Library Association, 2003).

6. Marilyn Elias, "Electronic World Swallows Up Kids' Time, Study Finds," *USA Today*, March 10, 2005, p. A.1.

7. Sven Birkerts, "The Truth about Reading," *School Library Journal*, Nov. 2004.

Chapter 3

THE IMPORTANCE OF LITERATURE IN THE SCHOOL LIBRARY

UNDERUTILIZED HAVENS: MIDDLE AND HIGH SCHOOL LIBRARIES

The library is the natural conduit to deliver books to the reader and share information with faculty members. Librarians have a sixth sense for knowing the stories that their patrons will love. They have an uncanny ability to spirit the perfect story into a reader's life. As the "specialist" in the realm of children's and young adult (YA) literature, our mission is to get the best titles out of the library and into busy lives.

As educational trendsetters, schools need to popularize the act of reading with the same aggressive energy they apply toward technological advancement. Parents should be weighing-in a school's educational potential by focusing on progressive literature programs. In reality, literature programs are few and far between. Underutilizing the school library's collection is the glaring weak link to developing a literature-enriched curriculum. While making room for technology, foreign language, advisor/advisee programs, upper-level math and science courses, and/or vocational educational programs, middle and high schools have squeezed reading instruction right out of the spectrum. There is little to no time for students to browse the library, and less for librarians to promote books. Uninformed, students have the wrong impression that there's nothing to read in the school library.

Even worse, while fretting about plummeting reading scores, secondary school educators are bypassing the most obvious part of balancing the equation: librarians. Why aren't school literature programs being developed? Why aren't they being expanded? Why aren't author visitations being heralded with the same enthusiasm as "going wireless"? Are educators falling into a rut, following along like lemmings, instead of recommending viable solutions and spearheading proactive measures? Administrators should be tapping into librarians' capabilities, aligning them with the English department, and scheduling time in the day for them to deliver instruction that will develop and forge a student's interest in literature.

It's true that children and young adults are reading much less than they once did. They're not finding it as attractive as the many other exciting media possibilities that surround us. The National Institute for Literacy summarized long-term reading assessments thus:

a smaller percentage of 13- to 17-year-olds read for fun daily in 1999 than in 1984;

a smaller percentage of 17-year-olds saw adults reading in their homes in 1999 than in 1984; and

a greater percentage of 17-year-olds were watching three or more hours of television each day in 1999 than in 1978.[1]

READING FOR PLEASURE

Librarians have access to book reviews and professional journals, are courted by book distributors, and attend conferences where publishers woo us with the newest titles. We've taken children's and YA literature courses. Simply put, librarians are the best faculty members to get the best literature into the forefront of the educational arena. In the hierarchy of the publishing profession, we're the ones connected to the audience. Having trendy displays in the library is not enough to get kids to read. Inspiring a child to embrace literature into their whole educational package adds unequivocal strength to their litany of communication skills. It's an instructional investment of time that has undeniable benefits. As Stephen Krashen writes, "Studies showing that reading enhances literacy development lead to what should be an uncontroversial conclusion: Reading is good for you. The research, however, supports a stronger conclusion: Reading is the only way, the only way we become good readers, develop a good writing style, an adequate vocabulary, advanced grammatical competence, and the only way we become good spellers."[2]

It is an ironic twist that reading for enjoyment receives low priority during the secondary school academic day. Scheduled library time, reading instruction, and/or literature appreciation classes are almost nonexistent. As educators, do we expect that students develop an appreciation of reading through osmosis? If time is allotted during the day for students to relax with a good book and/or magazine, they will. When I sense that the pace and energy of our school is getting too high, I'll ask my class, "Who would like to sit and read?" Aside from the unanimously positive response, you can almost hear a collective sigh of relief. In the frenzy of life, students need free-reading time built into their day.

Progressive administrators must look toward committing a segment of the academic day for students to use the library as a literary resource. Teaching to increase state standard and national achievement scores frustrates teachers, fails students, and places erroneous and erratic pressures on education. When school systems use a generic prescription to suit all students across the board, individual learning styles are cheated and creativity is stifled. Good decisions, commonsense practices, and implementation of sound programming get pushed aside. Trying to emphasize every discipline equally for all students ignores their needs and predilections. We know that for a large population of students, the discipline of reading—as a necessary skill of communication and comprehension—is undeveloped. Schools that provide free-reading "chill" time during the academic day encourage the appeal of reading to take root. Free-reading offers older students a chance to be exposed to, discover, and take advantage of literature that interests them. This makes good sense because children that read what they like, in turn, like to read.

Also, children who love to read often do so because somebody who loved to read shared that passion with them by reading aloud. The question is: Why do we ever stop reading stories out loud to our students? Reading aloud decreases in 5th and 6th grade and frequently ends just shy of middle school. Stories prove that we're not alone, and they share emotional depths passed over due to the speed of life. Why, at a time when students are vulnerable and thirsty for identity, would we eliminate this anchoring component from their educational package? Teenagers are easily fed-up with adult talk, yet they love hearing adults tell stories. If we stop telling children stories, we devalue the power, meaning, and importance of literature. Through omission, we contribute to indifference.

In Jack Humphrey's article "There Is No Simple Way to Build a Middle School Reading Program," he writes:

> Because reading achievement is the crucial link between middle school students and their future success, it is vital that middle schools provide the personnel, time and resources needed to produce successful readers. Middle school students should have the support of reading teachers every day, just as they are also engaged each day with teachers of English, mathematics, science, and social studies. Moreover, special attention from reading teachers should be given to those students who read two or more grade levels below their expected level. And because the school library is the logical place for students to find materials with which to practice their reading, middle schools need to ensure that students have access to new books, along with support from librarians.

He continues, "The school library is an indispensable partner for reading teachers. Reading is similar to athletics: students need to learn skills, but they must also continuously practice those skills. Many middle school students do not have access to books, magazines, and newspapers in their homes, and many more are from families that do not use public libraries. Fortunately, the school library is the one place where school districts can ensure that all students have access to current materials for independent reading."[3]

To offer the optimum use of the library, time must be sanctioned during the academic day for all students. It need not always be a planned time of instruction, but a time to luxuriate in focused moments, an oasis of undisturbed quiet within the perpetual sea of school-day chatter, a quiet moment to thumb through a magazine or read a book just for pleasure.

In discussing correlating research on reading achievement and literacy, Stephen Krashen writes, "Educators have no control over public libraries, no control over poverty, and no control over the price and availability of books in students' homes. But we have control over one source of books: SCHOOL."

Krashen continues, "The school library and classroom libraries can make a huge difference: The library can level the playing field and provide all children with a print-rich environment. All children will have the chance to do wide reading and grow in literacy, knowledge, and understanding. This is why the first step in all school reform must be improving school libraries."[4]

Reading is an interactive cerebral sport. If a student is unable to concentrate, unable to decode squiggly symbols into words—to conceptualize words into thoughts, envision thoughts into images and whole new worlds—well, without that cognitive ability, a student's intellectual freedom is impaired. On the educational shelf-life scale of what's useful and practical to access and retain, reading has a longevity that can't be beat. If students read for enjoyment, they'll enjoy that skill forever.

BUSTING "READING IS BORING" TO "READING ROCKS!"

Literature that endures the fickle fate of time wields artful and expressive language. Even so, there's no guarantee that it will survive the burgeoning and enticing electronic age, as the new generation's low reading scores and disinterest in the discipline attest. Today's students are opting for easier modes of communication. They consider reading boring and, unless shown otherwise, why wouldn't they?

School libraries have the depth of resources to revive despondent screen-fed children into curious independent thinkers. Getting books to spark a child's interest toward personal reflection, to cause a moment of pause, discomfort, or external awareness, is essential. The power of your library's collection provides the foundation. You and your faculty can provide the motivation. When children approach a book with the same open-mindedness they bring to a screen, a connection is made. Without that moment of willing inquisitiveness, literature is too quiescent to single-handedly make an impression. It needs help. Librarians may not be in control of changing pervasive social patterns, but we can disrupt and challenge them. We can open the library's floodgates and show busy students the appeal of literary exposure.

To convince children and teens that literature matters, parents and educators need to believe it does. If children are going to get the nuances and pleasures of literature, they need an introduction to tantalizing and captivating titles. If given administrative support, librarians, English teachers, and reading teachers will collaborate to encourage free-choice reading, knowing the end product will be students turned-on to reading.

Through booktalks and classes devoted to literature (see Reader's Workshop, Chapter 8), librarians will introduce secondary school students to the books they'll love. Students will be exposed to adventure stories that are captivating in their primitive hilarity, like Gary Paulson's autobiographical *How Angel Peterson Got His Name* (New York: Dell, 2003). Librarians can connect kids with witty and smart stories like Jack Gantos's "Jack Henry" series. Or titles that are poignant, eloquent, and soul-searching, like Sharon Creech's *Walk Two Moons* (New York: Scholastic, 1994). Titles that are brash, compelling, filled with conflict, and graced with multiple fresh voices, such as Chris Crutcher's *Ironman* (New York: Greenwillow, 1995), Nikki Grimes's *Bronx Masquerade* (New York: Dial, 2002), or David Levithan's *The Realm of Possibilities* (New York: Knopf, 2004) are particularly appealing. To convince students to step off the sidelines and engage in the action, introduce them to literature that speaks to them.

Interesting magazines will also convince students that reading is worth their time. A well-stocked YA book collection and magazine section will pull the most resistant and time-deprived students from the hallways, like the wafting aroma of baking brownies pulls them into the kitchen. For a comprehensive annotated list of contemporary magazines for middle and high school libraries, take a look at Julie Bartell's article "The Good, the Bad, and the Edgy" (*School Library Journal*, July 2005).

Stock your library with titles that contain funny, scary, and identifiable kid characters. Stock up on romance for teens, sci-fi, fantasy, adventure, and graphic novels. Stay a step ahead by being aware of (if not always understanding or condoning) kid culture. Introduce students and staff to such reads as *The Curious Incident of the Dog in the Night-time* or *The Lightening Thief* by Rick Riordan—before they become movies. Keep the collection teen-friendly.

LOGISTICS AND TIME MANAGEMENT

First and foremost, students need to have time to access the library during the day. They need free-reading time to enjoy the material that they *want* to read. Once that's done, here are some suggestions for increasing student awareness through collaborative efforts:

- Open the library before classes begin.
- Encourage students to visit the library during homeroom.
- Have the library open at the end of the academic day; this is particularly inviting during the drab, dark days of winter.
- Hold study halls in the library during the day, when students work on homework and/or have the opportunity for free independent reading. This is an advantageous time for a faculty member to help proctor the study hall, offering team-teaching potential, as well as quiet planning time. If I'm unable to secure faculty help, I use this time as sustained silent reading and/or studying—including myself in the group.
- Collaborate with the English faculty and teach a weekly literature appreciation class during English period (see Reader's Workshop, Chapter 8).
- Collaborate with the English faculty to teach a mini-unit on book reviewing.
- Hold booktalk sessions a few times a semester with English, humanities, and other classes.
- Facilitate a school book club during the arts elective block and offer academic credit.

It's essential to educate faculty about the newest titles for students. Again, the stumbling block will be finding time to do this. Encourage your administrator to let you host a booktalk session during faculty orientation days. If adults are introduced to the books, they'll get excited about them and get them to the students. For the adults who went ga-ga over Harry, he's just the beginning. Let them know about Phillip Pullman's *The Golden Compass* (New York: Dell Yearling, 1995), Neil Gaiman's *Coraline* (New York: HarperTrophy, 2004) and *Neverwhere* (New York: Perennial, 2003), and young Christopher Paolini's *Eragon* (New York: Random House, 2003) and *Eldest* (New York: Random House, 2005). Become a proponent of reading by plugging what's contemporary, interesting, and highly readable. Invite staff to share their favorite titles. Booktalks from the coolest adults in the school will fuel the popularity of catchy titles. The simplest things work. Seeing their teachers' enthusiasm about children's and YA titles will get students reading (see YA Literature to Grab Adults, Chapter 12).

The wheels of technology spin faster than a turbo merry-go-round, and educators are waging a dizzying effort to keep up. In this future of shifting rapids, channeling and harnessing the flow of information feels like a drowning prospect. Books capture content and present a solid foundation. While staying aware of a multitude of information resources, a librarian's unspoken professional responsibility is to stay aware of the best books. Keeping books in the forefront doesn't much matter if readers aren't in the flow. If students don't have the time to catch the pleasure of story, then as educators, we're drifting.

School librarians are in a catch-22 predicament. We want to promote the benefits and pleasures of reading for recreational enjoyment and intellectual enrichment; yet within the core curriculum there's a battery of material to be covered and research skills to be addressed and the reality is, there's scant room for literature.

The following chapters will offer you some innovative solutions to counteract this educational stalemate.

NOTES

1. National Environment for the Arts (NEA), "Reading at Risk: A Survey of Literacy Reading in America," Research Division Report 46, NEA report, 2002, p. 26.

2. Stephen Krashen, *The Power of Reading* (Westport, CT: Libraries Unlimited, 2004).

3. Jack W. Humphrey, "There Is No Simple Way to Build a Middle School Reading Program," *Phi Delta Kappan*, June 2002, Vol. 83, Iss. 10, p. 754.

4. Stephen Krashen, "What Do We Know about Libraries and Reading Achievement?" *Book Report*, Jan/Feb. 2002, Vol. 20, Iss. 4, p. 38.

Chapter 4

COOPERATIVE PLANNING

PROGRAM PLANNING WITH THE FACULTY

"Collaboration" is the academic buzz word these days, and it's a good one. Faculty members are encouraged to team-teach and collaborate, making this our time to take advantage of an invitation and turn it into a positive opportunity. A team player contributes to the overall cohesion of the team's working success. He or she doesn't run the show. It is important to strike a balance and know when to be a good listener and offer constructive feedback, and when to argue a position and carry the torch.

In order to maintain an overview of the faculty's programming needs—and see where your responsibilities lie and how your skills fit in—you'll need to objectively view the whole school's program. You will be able to augment curriculum needs effectively if you know what they are. This may require a bit of nosing about and inquiry. You will need to acquire characteristics like Radar's, from the old hit TV series *M.A.S.H.* That is, develop the omnipotent and unobtrusive quality of knowing what's going on in any given classroom up and down the hallways. Honing in on bits of information will contribute toward supporting the faculty's program and will make you an indispensable team partner. Team meetings are a means to this end.

Sometimes you have to do things that cause you discomfort because you know that the alternative is ugly. Like going to the dentist, the outcome is for the better, dealing with problems and gaining a sparkling smile. I hate attending team meetings. With a boatload of work haunting me, another meeting feels like an insurmountable interruption in the day. Yet I know that team meetings are the best way to stay abreast of day-to-day classroom happenings. Not attending team meetings separates you from the communication pool—an ineffectual spot for the "information specialist" to be.

Team meetings precipitate collaborative programming and encourage cooperative planning. Consider the team meeting the beginning, like the Table of Contents of a book. It offers a quick overview of the independent classrooms' contents. It's the time for you and your coworkers to collaboratively work up an outline. Collectively, you'll look at classroom themes, upcoming events, extra class visits, and booktalk new titles, as well as offer research support to faculty members. This is not the time to be tangentially creative but rather to absorb the collective ideas discussed. Assess the content of the meeting and follow up with faculty members to input subheading ideas and collaboratively write up chapter content.

An example of such a collaborative endeavor was when our 6th-grade English and history teacher was eager to immerse literature into her whole curriculum. She had been an active participant in our schoolwide reading program. We wanted to braid our separate programs, strengthening and enriching the instructional clout of each. The following model shows the power of such collaboration.

A COLLABORATIVE MODEL FOR 6TH GRADE

The 6th-grade teacher was determined to saturate literature into her classroom. She valued the library's reading incentive program and wanted her students to take advantage of it. At the end of the year we brainstormed how to mesh our programs for the following school year. We took several of our current programs and built upon their themes.

First we brought the library's whole-school reading incentive program into her classroom (see Title Trekking, Chapter 7). She introduced it to her students as part of their daily program and encouraged students to read at least one Title Trek prior to winter break. It would be their free-read, over and above the class assignments.

Then we looked at her customized sustained silent reading time, called "T"-Time—symbolizing: Take Time To Title Trek. Running with the "T"-Time idea, her classroom shelves held Title Treks those students checked out from the library. The teacher sprang random "T"-Times on the kids during the day. She would stand quietly at the front of the room, making the standard timeout hand signal used on the game field. Students would slowly notice, and quickly grab their books. In addition to serving the purpose of getting kids reading during the day, the students also kept an attentive eye on her. No student wanted to be last to notice the shift and be caught without a book. It was a fun interruption, and reading became a positive escape from the general academic routine. Imagine that!

Our initial partnership developed into designing a literary circle that joined two 6th-grade English classrooms from different schools. First we hosted a joint faculty meeting, inviting teachers from each school to collaborate ideas on curriculum theme, title choices, and a customized literary circle format. This evolved into hosting a literary "T"-Time with our neighboring school three times a year.

We began within our separate classroom circles before we merged the two classes. We alternated hosting the "T"-Times between the two schools and met in the library. Books were selected that had themes of survival—emotional and physical journeys. This merged well with the 6th-grade curriculums. Each class was split into three different literary circles, reading three different titles, comparing similar and contrasting themes. The two classes mirrored their title choices within their distinct and separate literary circles.

At our school, we also linked the library's literary appreciation class to corroborate the survival and journey themes of the 6th-grade class. We used segments from Jack Gantos's *Jack Adrift: Fourth Grade without a Clue* (New York: Farrar, Straus and Giroux, 2003) and *Jack on the Tracks: Four Seasons of Fifth*

Grade (New York: Farrar, Straus and Giroux, 1999) as companion novels to underscore these themes (see Reader's Workshop, Chapter 8). Jack was our school's visiting author that year, so this contributed to preparing for his visit.

Preselected titles that emphasized survival were placed on display in the library. Students selected a free-reading Title Trek that matched up with their literary circle theme. They were well prepared for classroom "T"-Time. At any given time the teachers would give the "T"-Time signal and students would drop everything to read their novel for 10–15 minutes.

The classes prepared for six weeks prior to coming together. They were more than ready when they met for a full afternoon and were grouped into three expanded literary circles. The teachers selected the students in each group, making sure there was a balance of strong readers and those challenged. Also, a mix of strong leaders and quiet participants contributed to the vitality of the group. Some ice-breaking introductory games were played. Each group was presented with a written question that they needed to answer together. For instance, "Describe the conflict that the main character is dealing with," or "Describe the resolution to the story." Open-ended questions were used to begin a healthy batch of dialogue. These questions prompted students to springboard into in-depth conversations.

Each literary circle had poster board, colored pencils, and markers. Working together on an illustrative poster of their novel helped dissolve social awkwardness. The teachers and the librarian circulated around, facilitating the circles and offering support. Students were encouraged to converse without restrictions. At the end of the work session, students from each group gave a brief booktalk and poster presentation to the rest of the class.

In addition to the excitement of bringing two classes together, meeting new peers, and enjoying a kind of field trip to the other school, another "carrot" was a social teatime held after the literary circle work sessions. Lots of tea biscuits, cookies, decaf flavored teas, and juice were served. Set a tray of delectable cookies in front of a bunch of hungry boys, and look out! Students were coached that teatime in England is as much of a display of refined and delicate manners as it is a time of yummy delicacies. Watching the students exaggerate snooty teatime manners beat watching them upstage one another's best hog tendencies.

There were three other major collaborative events that brought students to a heightened level of engagement: a presentation from our school's Korean students, reading a novel from a visiting author, and inviting an author to be our teatime guest.

A KOREAN EXCHANGE

Because there were two Korean students in our 6th-grade class, and because the collective curriculum theme revolved around ancient history, diversity, quests, journeys, and survival, the two classes selected Linda Sue Park's *A Single Shard* (New York: Clarion Books, 2001) for their first book. Our ten Korean English speakers of other languages (ESL) students, in 4th grade to 9th grade, read *A Single Shard* with their teacher. When the classes came together for a "T"-Time literary circle, our Korean students joined us. They were eager to have the tables turned, and they proudly shared some information about their homeland with their American classmates.

Putting on a presentation for the two 6th-grade classes, the ESL students described their personal knowledge of the history of the ancient Korean celadon glazing technique, brought in ceramic examples, wore the traditional dress used during festive occasions, held up maps to point out the cities where their families lived, and showed the ancient area Tree Ear (of *A Single Shard*) was from. An older Korean student even entertained the 6th-graders with some storytelling. For the social teatime, students served some traditional sesame and poppy-seed honey-laced pressed cookies. It was an exotic literary and cultural exchange.

COLLABORATING FOR AN AUTHOR VISIT

Our second group novel was Jack Gantos's *Joey Pigza Swallowed the Key* (New York: Farrar, Straus and Giroux, 1998). This choice further prepared students for his visit later in the year. There are many themes for a 6th-grade class to identify with in Joey Pigza, from bullying, to impulsivity, to learning disabilities, to dysfunctional families. Joey's life was a journey of self-awareness. We had lots of Joeys in our combined 6th-grade classes. The students' literary circles generated their own conversation and compassion, and required little input from the adults.

The collective literary circles followed the usual format described above. We saved the students' artwork and laminated the posters to decorate the library's bulletin board for Jack's visit.

Our school's 6th-graders made invitations that they sent to the other class, inviting them to visit when Jack Gantos presented. Unfortunately, between the best-laid plans of teachers and librarians—and life in the North Country—Jack arrived in January, when temperatures plummeted to 30 degrees below zero (the wind chill was 80 below). At a farm school frigid temperatures only make life harder. The horses, cows, and chickens must be tended and school goes on. Jack bravely and gamely forged northward. Unfortunately the public schools were closed due to the weather, and therefore our neighboring student guests missed out. We tried to reduce their disappointment by asking Jack to sign their paperback copies of *Joey Pigza Swallowed the Key*.

"T"EA TIME WITH AN AUTHOR

The culminating event to wrap-up the "T"-Time year was inviting author Tim Wynne-Jones to a social tea in the library. To get ready for his visit, we read several stories from Tim's short story collection *Some of the Kinder Planets* (New York: Orchard Books, 1995). We discussed them in our now well-established literary circles. One class had become so competent and comfortable with the "T"-Time experience, they entertained the author and the rest of the group with a reader's theater rendition of Tim's play *A Mad House*.

Ending the instructional reading and analysis of literature with some social interaction and tangible instruction made these novels and short stories memorable for these 6th-grade classes. The program extended through the year, creating a routine structure and establishing a pattern. Students became comfortable with joining and reconvening with another class. They learned to make good use of their limited time together, as well as experienced how to be hosts and behave as guests.

Most important, they discovered that literature lives outside the confines of the page through dynamic group interaction. As faculty members we learned that collaborative planning ignites individual ideas. Our separate parts came together, collaborating into tangible, vital, and meaningful instruction for our students. We were all energized from the success of the experience.

MULTICULTURAL LITERATURE AND COLLABORATION

A second example of collaborative programming is when I joined three faculty members to write up a grant proposal for a multicultural literature program. (I can't say enough positive things about grants—free money motivates you to document and articulate innovative educational programming designs that may be implemented at some future date with, or without, the grant. So, what's to lose?)

Our boarding farm school's population is a wonderful composite: 25 percent of our population is international and 12 percent are students of color. We hail from inner and international cities, from full-tuition scholarships and alums who donate millions of dollars to support the school. We're a natural for multicultural literary exchanges.

As a staff committee, we developed a year-long program that immersed the library's strong collection of multicultural titles into the 6th-, 7th-, and 9th-grade English curriculums. We wanted to expose students to cultural diversity and the cultures-within-cultures that can be seen within the United States. We ordered classroom sets of specific titles to explore themes of inner city and Native American culture.

The 9th-grade English curriculum theme was: "In Their Own Voices: How Does an Author's Life Experiences Shape His/Her Literary Voices?" This meshed with the coordinating theme of multicultural literature and our author visits that year: Janet McDonald, who grew up in the projects of Brooklyn, New York, and James Bruchac, a descendent of the Native American Abenaki Nation.

The 9th grade read all four of Janet McDonald's novels in a literary circle format. They read four shorts stories from a Latina collection that I brought back from the American Library Association conference. They also studied American poetry with a focus on diversity: Cultural, gender, and economic, from Walt Whitman through the Harlem Renaissance. The class performed a Harlem Renaissance monologue, showcasing individual personalities of the time. An open mike was set up in the classroom for biweekly student poetry readings.

The 6th-grade class read *Spellbound* (New York: Farrar, Straus and Giroux, 2001), beginning it in their Reader's Workshop class and then continuing reading independently. Most of them disliked the novel. This initial impression shifted when they met the author and were able to discuss the character's situation and empathize with the real-life ghetto lifestyle.

The 6th-grade class also read several of James Bruchac's Native American tales: *When the Chenoo Howls* (New York: Walker, 1998), *Native American Games & Stories* (Golden, CO: Fulcrum Kids, 2000), and *How the Chipmunk Got His Stripes* (New York: Dial, 2001). This class, in conjunction with their survival theme, was going on a three-day wilderness survival trip. We integrated James's

Adirondack wilderness training and national animal tracking expertise into the mix. James spent one day giving storytelling presentations to the whole school. His second day was spent with the 6th grade, in a half-day tracking and wilderness survival workshop. The other half of day James spent with the 7th-grade class, whose year-long English, history, and science concentration is Adirondack geography.

As the librarian, you may not be able to collaborate individually with every faculty member's programming, but you'll probably be able to accent and tweak your colleagues' programming by recommending supplementary curriculum materials. I've yet to meet a coworker who turns down support. More likely, they will appreciate your interest and respect your input.

Let's get back to the analogy of the Table of Contents and team meetings. From a self-perpetuating vantage point, attendance at team meetings will draw attention toward the library's literature programs. Being a team player does not guarantee that your colleagues will choose to play on your team. They may have a problem with fitting in another educational program. But by calling it to their attention, they just might consider it.

Keep an eye on the overall educational demands when introducing new program designs. Programming must be simple and do-able to encourage faculty to sample the idea. The program's longevity will build upon a well-informed staff that has confidence in your well-thought-out professional plan. Like going to the dentist, team meetings are worth the pain and the investment.

FREE-READING COSTS TIME

It will be up to your faculty if they want to etch time into the daily program for free-reading time. When you discuss the possibility, have some clear options available. Collaboration isn't always a brainstorming session. It can be bringing do-able suggestions before a group and then working them out into an agreeable and customized arrangement together.

Expecting students to read without guidelines is expecting a lot. Have you ever watched kids organize a team game on their own? Those teams are not likely to achieve cohesive longevity. Somebody's left out, a fight transpires, kids drop out of the mix, and the game dwindles to quits. Bring a coach into the fray and establish rules, and organization falls into place. Players take their position, the flak stops, and the game is played. By establishing concrete guidelines and becoming invested in the fact that reading during the school day matters, we convince students that it does. Dedicating time and structure to our convictions will make or break silent reading programs.

Two examples of implementing reading into the schedule in a comfortable, practical, and beneficial manner follow.

HOMEROOM OR MORNING MEETING TIME

Homeroom or morning meeting time is traditionally spent reviewing the day's events and provides time for students to get organized and centered before their day begins. It offers an excellent opportunity for some quiet reading. Free-reading will become a natural progression of the daily routine. Encourage faculty to stock their classroom bookshelves with interesting high-appeal kid titles and donate old magazines from the library.

Springing new programming on unsettled teens can have iffy consequences. Introduce shifts in the daily routine in a slow, systematic, and considerate manner. Changes should make sense, appeal to their interest, and attract their investment. The onus of reading as "work" needs to be diminished and the pleasurable aspects increased. Fun and humor are great magnets. So are fear and gore. Homeroom leaders need to make it clear from the get-go that this is reading time, not a study hall period to catch up on homework. It will take adjusting to, but once it has been established, it will become a welcome routine.

SILENT AND SPONTANEOUS READING

Our schoolwide reading incentive program is called Title Trekking, so we dubbed our customized sustained silent reading time as "T"-Time (Take Time To Title Trek). This program, started in the 6th-grade classroom (as described above) was then presented by that class to the whole school.

"T"-Time can happen anytime during the day, as long as it *happens*. It can be capitalized on for other purposes, like taking a quiet break during an unusually harried and frazzled day, or to celebrate a schoolwide reading activity during special library days such as the New York State Great Read Aloud Day or National Library Day. Have the principal announce "It's 'T'-Time!" over the loud speaker and watch everybody drop what they're doing and pick up their book. The surprise element captures attention. Teachers are rattled by the interruption; students love the distraction. It's a win-win for students. If they're reading, it's a win for teachers too.

Silent reading programs in elementary and middle schools should be a routine part of a student's educational package. These programs will set the stage for students to remain recreational reading participants as they progress through the upper grades.

LIBRARY, LITERACY, AND THE CURRICULUM

Implementing literature into the overall curriculum design reiterates instructional concepts. The design may fit in on a semester basis or over a full year. It will depend on your time and the academic schedule. It's a case where little is better than nothing.

Collaborative team meeting discussions will allow other faculty members to initiate their ideas and have input into the plan.

Here are some strategies to work the library's literature into the school day.

Language Arts Offer to take one period once a week, using a Reader's Workshop format (see Reader's Workshop, Chapter 8) to pair complementing literature and classroom themes. Select literary styles that are being taught within the class, but make sure they are kid-gripping. Read aloud examples from novels, short stories, poetry, and picture books. Choose material that you are familiar with and leave off at a point where students are begging to hear more. Time allotted: term or semester unit.

Humanities Offer to schedule a weekly class (see Reader's Workshop, Chapter 8) to coordinate classroom subject matter with the vast amount of historical fiction available. Here's just a sampling: *My Guardian Angel* by Sylvia Weil (New York: A.A. Levine, 2004) is an unusual tale steeped in Judaism—law and lore—about the Crusaders' assault on the Jewish villages in medieval France; *Out of the Dust* by Karen Hesse (New York: Scholastic, 1997) in which a tragic accident makes living in the dust bowl even more depressing; *Letters from Rifka*, also by Karen Hesse (New York: Henry Holt, 1992) in which a Jewish girl's immigration from Russia is fraught with tough times; *Lizzie Bright and the Buckminster Boy* by Gary Schmidt (New York: Clarion, 2004), set in 1911, on the beautiful coast of Maine, where community greed corrupts the peace and where an upstanding minister's son befriends a spunky African American girl; and *Dangerous Skies* by Suzanne Fisher Staples (New York: Farrar, Straus and Giroux, 1996), the suspenseful tale of friendship, murder, and accusations against an unjust storm of racism in the Chesapeake Bay area. Annotated bibliographies for historical fiction are plentiful. Time allotted: term or semester.

General Literature Classes/Reader's Workshop This is a team-teaching approach that encourages classes to visit the library once a week—extending beyond their research needs. With a self-contained classroom this may be offered throughout the year. For the upper grades, use a weekly slot during separate semester blocks, for example: 7th grade, one day a week throughout the fall; 8th grade, one day from mid-November through mid-January; and 9th grade, mid-January through spring break.

This class is a collaborative design working in conjunction with the upper-grade English curriculum. Faculty consultations are frequent, discussing where the class is, what they are concentrating on, and where they are headed. Though formal meetings take place during the semester, teachers are encouraged to discuss impromptu ideas as they occur. For instance, last year the 6th-grade English teacher was having trouble teaching her students about literary inferences. She asked me if I might work this into my Reader's Workshop class. Her request was simple to implement. Couched within reading an entertaining novel, her students were receptive to the instruction.

This deliberate scheduling maximizes the librarian's contact with all students and increases the odds of getting literature into the forefront of their awareness. It supports the curriculum's focus by concentrating on literary skills that underscore academic content and programming, that is:

SAT prep—reading comprehension, essay writing, and vocabulary

Increased examples of essay composition for secondary school and/or college applications

Reiterating literary terms and styles through examples from read-aloud selections

Poetry slams

Open mikes

Visiting Author Program preparation

Library literature programs offer students another environment and new content matter with which to explore and practice what they've been taught. Apprehension is reduced; comprehension is increased.

LITERACY AND NONFICTION

Librarians are not superhuman, but people who serve as resource lightening rods. We attract information. In our most effective state, we conduct information to the appropriate grounding source. It's not our mission to understand everything, but rather to disseminate the right information to the people who will understand it. As an information conduit we point faculty members toward professional resources to buck-up their curriculum. There are a number of reference titles that cover nonfiction cross-curricular subject matter and include annotated bibliographies. Two such titles are Kathleen Baxter's *Gotcha Again: More Nonfiction Booktalks to Get Kids Excited about Reading* (Westport, CT: Libraries Unlimited, 2002), and Beverly Kobrin's well used *Eyeopeners II: Children's Books to Answer Children's Questions about the World around Them* (New York: Scholastic, 1995).

We are the target of a load of brochures and catalogues from publishers. We're also the recipients of professional journals in which trends in education—particularly technology and literature—are highlighted. Knowing about all the trends, titles, and best teaching practices is useless if this knowledge is not imparted to the educational community. Professional articles and essays will often relate directly to a specific teacher's instructional unit. Faculty members will be especially appreciative of articles with accompanying thematic bibliographies. Count on their requesting some of the titles from these bibliographies. If you have access to *School Library Journal*'s, *Curriculum Connections*, pass it along to the faculty members that it best suits. *Curriculum Connections* coordinates topical literature with classroom instruction. Currently it is still free for the asking. If resources like *Curriculum Connections* aren't brought to the faculty's attention, they miss a big chunk of their intended audience.

I carry useful material to the staff meetings and hand it off to the appropriate faculty members. I also give a quick and enthusiastic verbal introduction to assure that it will be looked at. I may include a Post-It note with other staff names to whom it should be passed along. Pass out appropriate essays from professional journals. Mindful that boys love nonfiction, I brought along Michael Sullivan's "Why Johnny Won't Read: Schools Often Dismiss What Boys Like. No Wonder They're Not Wild about Reading"[1] to share. This commonsense no-nonsense article emphasizes the male attraction toward nonfiction reading. It can only affect core curriculum faculty if it's brought to their attention. Give it to them. Add a silly note to the science teacher like:

Todd,
I thought you might find this book on Phineas Gage[2] interesting. After an 1800s railroad explosion, poor Phineas stumbled around town with a 13-pound iron stake impaled in his skull! Inadvertently, he discovered the lobotomy. Let's get your class in for some other stranger-than-fiction nonfiction books.
Alison

Booktalking to the social studies and science curriculums will enrich the subject matter while simultaneously promoting reading. Hooking up biographies on explorers, political activists, scientists, inventors, athletes, and other innovative and pioneering personalities will captivate listeners. Bring along irresistible titles to show and tell, like James Solheim's *It's Disgusting and I Ate It! True Food Facts from Around the World and Throughout History* (New York: Simon & Schuster, 1998). There are so many entertaining and fascinating nonfiction books to provide additional fodder for a research/reading project. The one certainty is that they will be missed without an introduction.

AND LITERATURE FOR ALL

Place your collection into the hands of those who will use it most by staying tight with the language arts department. This is the department to align yourself with if you want to successfully launch your literature programs. If you pass along sure-thing titles to them, they will pass them on to their students. They'll also clue you in on their students' reading interests.

We have contact with students who read a lot. Our coworkers carry on the daily struggle with the students who don't. Many resistant readers feel an undercurrent of intellectual scorn, real or imagined. They avoid entering the library because they perceive it as an uninviting academic zone. Developing a strong professional relationship with the core teachers puts us in a better position to connect with these students. We can initiate conversations, welcome them into the library, and put interesting and highly readable material into their hands. If we're out of the network of those who need us most, we increase the probability that they'll fall through the cracks.

The librarian's and the teaching faculty's alliance will integrate literary sustenance into the core of the school. You have the resources and the knowledge of where, and how best, they will be used. Your coworkers have the students, a predetermined curriculum design, and most precious of all, time to teach (well, at least some time). Capitalizing on your individual strengths and pooling them together with a collaborative strategy will produce a creative and formidable team of educators. The idea of whole-language learning will achieve potent fruition with this partnership. Not taking advantage of collaborative, cooperative, and coordinating planning is to deprive your students of a stimulating education.

NOTES

1. Michael Sullivan, "Why Johnny Won't Read: Schools Often Dismiss What Boys Like. No Wonder They're Not Wild about Reading," *School Library Journal*, Aug. 2004, pp. 36–39.

2. John Fleischman, *Phineas Gage: A Gruesome but True Story about Brain Science* (Houghton Mifflin, 2002).

Part II

SETTING UP THE FOUNDATIONS
FOR LITERATURE PROGRAMS

Chapter 5

INTEGRATING LITERATURE INTO THE CURRICULUM

Faculty members tend to teach one book at a time in order to discuss theme and content within a group setting. This makes sense. It also makes sense to encourage a second selection with a complementary theme, similar subject matter, unusual writing styles, and distinguishing contemporary content. Librarians are the most knowledgeable resource to help English teachers select multiple titles with common or diverse themes, and differing reading challenges, that will be interesting and appealing to any student in the class.

Literary circles serve well to extend the one-book discussion into simultaneous discussions. There are a number of resources designed to help teachers implement literary circles within the classroom—this isn't one of them. Instead, the following information offers ideas and suggestions to supplement curriculum themes with enriching literature, in and out of the classroom. This is an opportunity to collaborate with faculty members, offering your input and assistance to broaden the literary choices in the classroom.

LITERARY GENRES AND THE CURRICULUM

POETRY

Occasionally there is an English teacher within the secondary school that is an expert in contemporary children's and young adult (YA) poetry. There may even be faculty members with a strong background in classical poetry. But by virtue of being every publisher's contact person, the librarian remains the best resource in the field. Librarians don't need to be experts on poetry, or any other subject or literary style for that matter, to be effective. Through careful scrutiny and selection, and by knowing our clientele, we acquire material that best serves the needs of the faculty and students. Like a high-end clothing boutique that caters to a shopper's delight, a successful collection will serve the faculty's instructional requirements while attracting the students' discerning eyes.

Shel Silverstein (*Where the Sidewalk Ends*, New York: Harper & Row, 1974, and *Falling Up*, New York: Harper & Collins, 1996) is a poet the kids know and love. Many children are introduced to his material before elementary school. Suggest that your faculty build on familiarity. Poetry is many things, including rhythm, repetition, and reflection. Reintroduce Robert Louis Stevenson's

A Child's Garden of Verses (New York: Golden Press, c1978) or a children's poetry anthology like *Wider Than the Sky: Poems to Grow Up With*, edited by Scott Elledge (New York: HarperCollins, 1990). Edward Lear's *Complete Nonsense Book* (New York: Dodd, Mead, 1962, c1912) of poetry, limericks, and fairy tales is another good opening. Then proceed to today's poetry that deals with teen and contemporary issues: Naomi Shahib Nye's *19 Varieties of Gazelle: Poems of the Middle East* (New York: Greenwillow, 2002), or Naomi Shahib Nye and Paul Janeczko's collection of over 200 poems, *I Feel a Little Jumpy Around You: A Book of Her Poems and His Poems Presented in Pairs* (New York: Simon & Schuster Books for Young Readers, 1996), in which male and female poets see the same topics presented in pairings that offer insight into how men and women look at the world, both separately and together.

Encourage teachers to sign out poetry collections and set up a display in their classroom. Inevitably, as soon as one faculty member signs out a bunch of poetry books, there will be another class, from another grade, right behind them, hell-bent on studying poetry. In fact, there may be several other classes. It's an educational phenomenon. The good news is that students often balk at poetry, and you'll be able to change this, giving them the best material that is sure to be a hit. Here are some strategies to answer the instructional demands:

Pull still more poetry titles off the shelves and divvy them up for different classes.

Take a moment to seek out and have conversations with the respective teachers. Inform them of what the other teachers are doing. Two things will happen: The dual interest compounds demand and makes poetry irresistibly desirable and, the teachers, from different grades and opposite ends of the building, will begin talking to one another about what they are teaching. They will share ideas, brainstorm, and plan. They may invite an upperclassman in to read poetry to the younger classmen and vice versa. They may host a special poetry slam or an evening open mike session. Best of all, they'll plan intelligent and collaborative instruction, as opposed to teaching in independent isolation.

Collect poetry into a binder that is tailor-made for curriculum needs. When attending team meetings, ask coworkers for copies of the poems that they are using in their classes. Let them know that you are collecting them for future use. Keep the binder in a central location. Make certain that every poem has the proper credit and/or bibliographic citation. Staff members on the run (and aren't we all?) will be able to borrow the binder to use it in their classes, or borrow it overnight to lead them toward other anthologies to pursue.

Find out what poets the students are studying so you can pass along biographical information or, better yet, encourage students to find it.

Maintain a collection of poetry that you feel will suit the language arts curriculum needs and add it to the binder.

Using poetry in nontraditional areas is possible and plausible. When the English department is studying poetry, help them collaborate with the science and history departments and saturate poetry into the curriculum. Advanced team planning and collaboration will assure that this happens. Steer faculty members toward popular material that has hit the scene. Poetry is a refreshing change of pace.

Consider the following titles for science, history, life skills or cultural arts units:

Forian, Douglas. *Omnibeasts*. Orlando, FL: Harcourt, 2004.

Greenberg, Jan. *Heart to Heart: New Poems Inspired by Twentieth-Century American Art*. New York: Abrams, 2001.

Grimes, Nikki. *Tai Chi Morning: Snapshots of China*. Chicago: Cricket, 2004.

Katz, Susan. *A Revolutionary Field Trip: Poems of Colonial America*. New York: Simon & Schuster, 2004.

Myers, Walter Dean. *Here in Harlem: Poems in Many Voices*. New York: Holiday House, 2004.

Myers, Walter Dean. *Blues Journey*. New York: Holiday House, 2003.

Nelson, Marilyn. *Fortune's Bones: The Manumission Requiem*. Asheville, NC: Front Street, 2004.

Nelson, Marilyn. *Carver: A Life in Poems*. Asheville, NC: Front Street, 2001.

Panzer, Nora. *Celebrate America: In Poetry and Art*. New York: Hyperion, 1994.

Scieszka, Jon, and Lane Smith. *Science Verse*. New York: Viking, 2004. It's funny, informative, and comes with a CD of Scieszka reading his poetry.

Singer, Marilyn. *Central Heating: Poems about Fire and Warmth*. New York: Random House, 2004.

NOVELS-IN-VERSE, JOURNALS, AND LETTERS

Poetry, journals, a mix of letters and narrative, and free-thought creative writing combine to present a rich selection of original styles. Because of their relatively new-book-on-the-block format, you'll have to call them to your faculty's attention and show them how to use them. Ed Sullivan's article "Fiction or Poetry?" describes the power of these poetic gems:

> Novels in verse can be an appealing, accessible introduction for students turned off by poetry or reluctant to read it. The verse authors write for these books is not like what most students are forced to study in class—it does not require analysis and explication. It is straightforward, but it retains the rhythm and succinctness of traditional poetry.... There is also a more practical attraction for students—novels in verse are a shorter and faster read. The substantial white space on the pages appeals to reluctant readers.[1]

Share with your faculty new ways to integrate these titles into the program. Our 8th- and 9th-grade English classes use Nikki Grimes's *Bronx Masquerade* (New York: Dial, 2002) to inspire students to host weekly open mike sessions. Novels-in-verse (NIV) beg for classroom use. You'll soon be linking these works to the curriculum as solidly as you do standard novels.

NOVELS-IN-VERSE: AN ANNOTATED BIBLIOGRAPHY

Cleary, Beverly. *Dear Mr. Henshaw*. New York: Scholastic, 1983. Through letters to his favorite author a young boy copes with his parents' divorce and other disasters, like having his lunch stolen, humor, and resolution. Girls and boys love this book. (grades 4th–6th)

Cormier, Robert. *Frenchtown Summer*. New York: Delacorte, 1999. The master of raw reality takes on a voice of nostalgic sensitivity. Lyrical vignettes offer powerful 1938 reminiscences of family, hot summer times, and missing a father away at war. (grades 5th–high school [HS])

34   Reviving Reading

Creech, Sharon. *Heartbeat*. New York: HarperCollins, 2004. This deals with friendship, life cycles, and individualism. (grades 4th–8th)

Creech, Sharon. *Granny Torrelli Makes Soup*. New York: Scholastic, 2003. Tender generational stories. Best friendships endure the test of time, and jealousy. (grades 6th–8th)

Creech, Sharon. *Love That Dog*. New York: Harper Trophy, 2001. This is the NIV to have the boys begging for more. (grades 4th–6th)

Crist-Evans, Craig. *North of Everything*. Cambridge, MA: Candlewick, 2004. This deals with the themes of relocating, death, and assuming difficult family responsibility in a rural landscape. (grades 6th–8th)

Crutcher, Chris. *Ironman*. New York: Greenwillow Books, 1995. This one is a blend of letters within a novel on friendships, athletics, anger management, and resolution. (grades 8th–HS)

Cushman, Karen. *Catherine, Called Birdy*. New York: Clarion, 1994. Journal entries of our plucky young narrator in medieval times provide a hilarious take on being betrothed to an old man with bugs in his beard. The flip side of a princess's diary, this is a teen's disparaging view of castle life. (grades 4th–7th)

Danziger, Paula, and Ann M. Martin. *P.S. Longer Letter Later*. New York: Scholastic, 1998. Two friends who are very different—one flamboyant, the other conservative—stay in touch through their letters. Girls love this book. (grades 4th–7th)

Frost, Helen. *Keesha's House*. New York: Farrar, Straus and Giroux, 2003. Hardships, homelessness, and unconditional friendships unite to form a tight surrogate family—healthy, supportive, and hopeful. (grades 7th–HS)

Grimes, Nikki. *Bronx Masquerade*. New York: Dial, 2002. Eighteen teen voices speak their souls and reveal their poetic mix of differences. This is an excellent choice for a multicultural unit and to spark creative writing. (grades 7th–HS)

Hesse, Karen. *Out of the Dust*. New York: Scholastic, 1997. This 1929 story of dust bowl Depression years includes family hardships, poetry, and heart-wrenching pathos. (grades 5th–8th)

Johnson, Angela. *Gone from Home: Short Takes*. New York: DK Ink/A Richard Jackson, 1998. This is a book of sparse and lovely prose that teens immediately relate to. (grades 6th–9th)

Levithan, David. *The Realm of Possibility*. New York: Random House, 2004. This work on friendships, romance, and teen sexuality is a knock-out! (grades 8th–HS)

Merrill, Billy. *Talking in the Dark*. New York: Scholastic/Push Cart, 2003. Poetry memoir, family relationships, homosexuality. Poignant and painfully beautiful. (Reproduced, with permission, from *School Library Journal* Copyright © by Reed Business Information A division of Reed Elsevier Inc. A. Follos. *School Library Journal*, Jan. 2004, Vol. 50, Iss. 1, p. 168.) (grades 8th–HS)

Nelson, Marilyn. *Carver*. Asheville: Front Street, 2001. George Washington Carver comes to life through the poetic voices of a multitude of observers. It's as evocative as it is informative. (grades 6th–HS)

Wolff, Virginia Euwer. *Make Lemonade*. New York: Henry Holt, 1993. This title is one of the pioneer books in the NIV format. An unwed needy teen mother, a baby, a toddler, and a compassionate 14-year-old babysitter help heal the hurts that accompany the ebb and flow of desperation. (grades 6th–9th)

Woodson, Jacqueline. *Locomotion*. New York: Putnam, 2003. A fire takes his parents, a stranger's home absorbs his sister, and he feels abandoned in a foster home. Lonnie begins to feel—and tell—about flickers of hope and light that embrace him—really sad and really joyful. (grades 5th–8th)

NOVELS

When language arts, social studies, and humanities classes join forces to spread a common theme throughout the grade level, the time is ripe for complementing literature. Put the antennae up, tune in, and give up the goods. This is the perfect opportunity to share the power of literature and link the library's stronghold with curriculum needs.

Historical novels on the Holocaust, the American Revolution, the Harlem Renaissance, and civil rights in the 1960s are just some of subject matter sought. The prevalent amount of great titles to buddy-up with these subjects is practically endless. Your immediate knowledge and available resources will be your only limits. Utilize review and annotation resources to broaden the scope. Rely on interlibrary loan to bulk-up the collection without depleting the budget.

Some schools have "life skills" classes that tackle teen issues like pregnancy, abuse, homelessness, eating disorders, running away, and suicide. These classes are always seeking thematic novels on survival, physical and emotional journeys, bullying, heroes, substance and emotional abuse, and a multitude of other teen-related subjects. Increasingly, YA titles are confronting controversial and non-traditional battles. The range of mature material is intense, and you will need to keep tabs on it. As far as hooking up to books with radical subject matter, it gets easier all the time.

Do the legwork. Pull novels and invite faculty members to bring in their classes. Have thematic titles on display and booktalk them in a short and engaging manner. Prepare and print coordinating title and author lists in advance. During your booktalks, students and faculty can check off the titles they are interested in revisiting after your presentation. Be prepared for students to act like they've never heard a word you've said. They'll rush you, pleading, "Which one will I like?" As maddening as this will be, breathe deeply. With their reliance comes faith and a developing trust for your recommendations. They've silently ordained you as the person who knows just what they'll want to read. They think that you've read every book in the library! Take the honor graciously and guide them to the books. This is what joy is all about: having students excited about reading.

Librarians absorb trivia through the nature of our daily interactions and exposure; we accumulate random information like a desk collects clutter. Share interesting background tidbits about authors. Faculty members love trivia that relates to the novels they're using in class. Simplifying their research is invaluable. Coworkers will pick your brain—stay inviting and be generous.

Share appropriate professional reference resources with your faculty. Again, *School Library Journal*'s *Curriculum Connections* is an excellent choice. Also, Scarecrow Press[2] offers secondary school literature guides with accompanying annotated bibliographies on the following subjects: Middle Ages, the Holocaust, health of native people, colonial America, and World War II. It also has a title that tackles multicultural themes of diversity that extend beyond multiethnicity to encompass nontraditional families, mental or physical illnesses, homosexuality, and abuse.

I am shying away from supplying a list of novels—it could be another book. Refer to the North Country School Title Trek list for forty-six contemporary titles for students from 4th grade through HS (see Title Treks, Chapter 7).

THEIR OWN VOICE: AUTHOR AUTOBIOGRAPHIES

Clue language arts faculty in to the proliferation of author autobiographies. Not only are YA author autobiographies on the rise, but publishers are also pumping out biographical series on children's and YA authors. As the purveyors and collectors of material, librarians are well aware of how full this market has become. Help to integrate biographical titles into the curriculum, linking them with literary units studying the particular author's work, or the genre that an author has been credited with defining.

Author autobiographies may be one of the best examples for students learning how to assert their own voices. Authors have a knack for presenting real information imbued with embellishments. Distinctive snapshots of engaging literary styles jazz up ordinary real-life events. Through example, students will grasp the oblique meaning of "writing what they know." Many authors use the journal and/ or memoir style for recording their lifetime antics and experiences. Encourage faculty members to capitalize on this. Faculty should highlight the advantages of daily journal entries from which to later pull ideas. This is an excellent form in which to motivate students to record their thoughts.

Finally, it should be noted that though there are a great number of YA author autobiographies that center on the authors' youth and coming-of-age teen years, there are many others, dealing with a lifetime of material, that are most appropriate for high school students.

Author autobiographies and biographies are a strong link for thematic units. They'll reach beyond the language arts curriculum to entice the social studies, sciences, and humanities departments with biographies about leaders, athletes, inventors, scientists, and other major players in the field. Having students read a biography throughout a semester unit works in concert with a culminating research paper. The trick is to have students select a personality with whom they are particularly interested. To make this happen, present animated book talks on carefully chosen, high-quality selections.

Here are just a few selections for linking authors with a time period and those whose life experiences centered on particular social and/or cultural issues:

DIVERSITY

Cary, Lorene. *Black Ice*. New York: Random House, 1991. A young African American woman leaves her black suburban Philadelphia neighborhood to become one of the first females and black students in an elite and predominantly white New Hampshire boarding school. She grows up and returns as a teacher. Inspirational. (HS–adult)

Hurston, Zora Neale. *Dust Tracks on a Road: An Autobiography*. New York: HarperTrade, 1996. After 62 years her voice still exceeds the standard. Her ability to capture folklore, vernacular, and dialect, and to celebrate her own mind sings out strong and genuine; a showcase of the timeless influence of brilliant writing. (HS–adult)

McDonald, Janet. *Project Girl*. New York: Farrar, Straus and Giroux, 1999. From the Projects to the Ivy League, this memoir exposes the underlying truths corroding the façade of a charmed life. Survival and great achievements. (HS–adult)

Myers, Walter Dean. *Bad Boy*. New York: HarperCollins, 2001. From a downtrodden Harlem neighborhood, this bad boy makes good. Blessed with gifts but racked with self-doubt, he rises above obstacles to nab his gift of expression. (7th–HS)

COMING-OF-AGE, FAMILY HISTORY, AND MEMOIRS

Alpett, Kathi. *My Father's Summers, A Memoir*. New York: Henry Holt, 2004. The 1960s are portrayed loudly and clearly. That era permeates this story as thoroughly as does the love of her dad—absent from home—but always present in her life. Infused with the rich and piquant nostalgia of a little girl. (grades 6th–adult)

Crutcher, Chris. *King of the Mild Frontier*. New York: Greenwillow, 2003. A natural storyteller who grew into his gift, he expresses his seemingly normal childhood coupled with the idiosyncrasies that make life real. (grades 6th–HS)

Feltcher, Ralph. *Marshfield Dreams: When I Was a Kid*. New York: Henry Holt, 2005. Despite the disruption of a move, this boy has an idyllic family life stuffed with love and nature. (grades 6th–8th)

Gantos, Jack. *Hole in My Life*. New York: Farrar, Straus and Giroux, 2002. In search of muse and money, this dream of riches sinks when the young writer ends up busted. At once honest, scary, funny, and inspirational. (grades 7th and up)

Giff, Patricia Reilly. *Don't Tell the Girls*. New York: Holiday House, 2005. Tracing family roots, having allegiances with our grandparents, and uncovering the mysteries of our ancestors. If you're dogmatic, you can find out. (grades 5th–7th)

Paulsen, Gary. *How Angel Peterson Got His Name*. New York: Wendy Lamb, 2003. The hilarious antics of a group of 13-year-old boys' harebrained schemes gone awry. (grades 6th–8th)

Paulsen, Gary. *Eastern Sun, Winter Moon: An Autobiographical Odyssey*. New York: HarcourtBrace, 1993. Life in the Philippines when the author's care is supervised by adult instability, promiscuity, and the rage of war. (HS–adult)

Zindel, Paul. *The Pigman and Me*. New York: Charlotte Zolotow, 1991. The author's life when he found, emulated, and later immortalized, his own pigman. Rich and funny. (grades 7th–HS)

TRAVEL LOG

Grimes, Nikki. *Tai Chi Morning*. Chicago: Cricket, 2004. Part travel journal, poetry reflections, and illustrations of the land by China's native son, Ed Young. (grades 4th–8th)

COLLECTIONS/SKETCHES

Gallo, Donald, ed. *Speaking for Ourselves, Autobiographical Sketches by Notable Authors of Books for Young Adults*. Urbana, IL: NCTE, 1990. A noteworthy collection of essays from, and about, some of our best-known YA authors. (grades 6th–HS)

SHORT STORIES

Most English teachers introduce short stories at some point. And it's good that they do. Short stories, because of their brevity, are a giant literary genre to which educators should pay serious attention. In our age of extrapolating too much information in too little time, the short story is a practical and functional literary format for readers. It can be the least intimidating and perhaps the most stylistically sophisticated expository prose. Collaboratively, it can be used in the study of creative writing or throughout the whole curriculum in multiple subject areas. There are so many great short story anthologies and collections—from yesterday's masters to today's contemporary YA authors—that your biggest difficulty will be in limiting the selection.

In Canadian children's and YA author Tim Wynne-Jones's essay on the power of literary brevity on today's young readers, he writes, "And Story will survive. But I suspect that the form may change—may have to change—to suit the temper of the time. For the child who is plagued by EDS (Electronic Diversion Syndrome), I can't help but think that shorter stories—good, pithy, exciting, funny and/or thought-provoking stories—may be all there is time for anymore."

He goes on, "That's what a short story can be: a literary black hole, dense and full of gravity. It is, in any case, a miniature. Not the whole journey, just a stop along the way. Not the whole season, just the big game. Not the whole sunset, just one straggler on the beach. . . . The short story does not presume to grandeur. It is happy to invoke a gasp of surprise, a belly laugh, a single tear."[3] The collaborative librarian will pass along such a definitive and comprehensive essay to faculty members. Then the librarian will offer up a wealth of short story collections and help plan how the teaching can be done.

A carefully selected short story of a high interest level for the young reader may be the first step in convincing a resistant reader that it's worth their effort. Its literary merit, practicality, and manageable amount of pages make it a receptive choice. The reader whose prime focus is flipping back and forth to see how many pages are left will thank you for a story they can finish with a sense of achievement and accompanying satisfaction. Use of the short story has the potential to promote literature that is strong, contemporary, and likely to get students interested in reading.

The large amount of short story collections being published makes this an opportune moment for the library to help revitalize the language arts department's selections. Many faculty members still lean on titles collected from their college literature and creative writing days. Good stuff no doubt, but it's time for them to bring new titles into their classrooms. Faculty members who attend conferences are introduced to new material, but the title pool is extensive and there is always room for more. The combination of selecting, purchasing, and reviewing children's and YA literature on a steady basis once again makes the librarian the point-person for staff to rely upon. Offer your services generously.

The following collections are just a few selections from the emerging and established masters of today's short stories:

SHORT STORIES: AN ANNOTATED BIBLIOGRAPHY

Appelt, Kathi. *Kissing Tennessee: And Other Stories from the Stardust Dance*. New York: Harcourt, 2000. Interrelated stories about individual teens preparing for their 8th-grade dance. Every story shifts imperceptibly through a radical range of teen and family issues. (Reproduced, with permission, from *School Library Journal* Copyright © by Reed Business Information A division of Reed Elsevier Inc. A. Follos. *School Library Journal*, Sept. 2000, Vol. 46, Iss. 9, p. 225.) (grades 5th–9th)

Barrett, Peter A., ed. *To Break the Silence: Thirteen Short Stories for Young Readers*. New York : Dell, c1986. Some of the best contemporary writers, including Philippa Pearce,

Walter D. Edmonds, E.L. Konigsburg, Langston Hughes, Katherine Paterson, Joan Aiken, and Howard M. Fast. (grades 7th–HS)

Carver, Peter, ed. *Close Ups: Best Stories for Teens*. Red Deer, Alta: Red Deer, 2000. Dotted with teen issues, stories are included that reflect an artful glimpse of historical eloquence captured to perfection; subtle, understated, and powered with meaningful moments. (Reproduced, with permission, from *School Library Journal* Copyright © by Reed Business Information A division of Reed Elsevier Inc. A. Follos. *School Library Journal*, Apr. 2001, Vol. 47, Iss. 4, p. 139.) (grades 7th–HS)

Crutcher, Chris. *Athletic Shorts*. New York: Greenwillow, 1991. Crutcher is the King of Issues. Here are stories about gender, abuse, racism, mental and physical disabilities, and sports—that rarely have to do with sports. Multiple themes and tangential experiences revisited from characters previously introduced in his novels. (grades 7th–HS)

Gallo, Donald, ed. *Destination Unexpected*. Cambridge, MA: Candlewick, 2003. This anthology is composed of stories in which the protagonists embark on journeys that are both literal and metaphorical; their physical progressions mirror inner transformations inspired by events big and small. (grades 5th–HS)

Gallo, Donald, ed. *No Easy Answers: Short Stories about Teens Making Tough Choices*. New York: Bantam Doubleday Dell, 1997. Stories that test the strength of a teen's ethical standards. Faced with blackmail, peer/parental pressures, drugs, unwanted pregnancy, and other real conflicts, teens face consequences and take responsibility for their actions. (grades 8th–HS)

Gallo, Donald, ed. *Join in Multiethnic Short Stories*. New York: Bantam Doubleday Dell, 1993. Views on acceptance, rejection, prejudice, expectations, and confrontations of young adults from a variety of ethnic backgrounds who just want to do the American teen thing: get a driver's license, go to college, play music, engage in sports, and fall in love. (grades 7th–HS)

Hemingway, Ernest. *The Nick Adams Stories*. New York: Scribner, reissue, 1981. A look into the "fictional" account of the author's life, adolescence through adulthood, filled with the outdoor passion and participation that infused his writing and the insidious suicidal depression that destroyed it. (HS)

Hurston, Zora Neale, adapted by Joyce Carol Thomas. *The Skull Talks Back*. New York: Harper Collins, 2004. Retelling of short and scary southern folktales. (grades 6th–HS)

Johnson, Angela. *Gone from Home*. New York: DK Ink, 1998. Mini-stories that are sparse, rich, and lyrical—a great example of writing in your own voice. (grades 5th–HS)

Levithan, David, ed. *Where We Are What We See*. New York: Scholastic/Push Cart, 2005. A collection of the best-of-the-best middle and high school prose, poetry, and fine art. An example to display exemplary young talent and to motivate the potential in your students. (grades 5th–HS)

Salisbury, Graham. *Island Boyz*. New York: Wendy Lamb, 2002. My favorites: "The Ravine," "Frankie Diamond Is Robbing Us Blind," and the "The Doi Store Monkey." Salisbury is a master of exposing the dark side of youth. A mix of first-person narratives that are rich in vernacular, drawing readers into exotic, and occasionally cataclysmic, island-life experiences. (Reproduced, with permission, from *School Library Journal* Copyright © by Reed Business Information A division of Reed Elsevier Inc. A. Follos. *School Library Journal*, Mar. 2002, Vol. 48, Iss. 3, p. 238.) (grades 7th–HS)

Singer, Marilyn (collected by). *Make Me Over*. New York: Dutton Children's, 2005. Eleven stories that are not the typical Hollywood fluff that captivates the girl, or boy, next door. Tough stuff, sweet stuff, and much of it good. (Reproduced, with permission, from *School Library Journal* Copyright © by Reed Business Information A division of Reed Elsevier Inc. (grades 6th–9th)

Moeyaert, Bart (translated from the Flemish). *Brothers.* Asheville, NC: Front Street, 2005. Forty-six personal vignettes, none longer than four pages, offer the timeless adventures, inherent security, and the sweet, pungent, and poignant experience of being the youngest of seven brothers. (Reproduced, with permission, from *School Library Journal* Copyright © by Reed Business Information A division of Reed Elsevier Inc. A. Follos. *School Library Journal*, Vol. 52, Iss. 1, p. 60.) (grades 5th–HS)

Salinger, J.D. *Nine Stories.* New York: Bantam, 1964. Fifty years after they were conceived, these characters still mirror the idiosyncrasies of the suburbanite. The portraits are touched with innocence and tipped by mental instability. (HS)

Stern, Jerome, ed. *Micro Fiction: An Anthology of Really Short Stories.* New York: W.W. Norton, 1996. The epitome of the profound profundity of a brilliant constructed *really* short story. Show students the power of placing few words, *just so*. (grades 4th–HS)

Young, Cathy. *One Hot Second: Stories about Desire.* New York: Knopf Books for Young Readers, 2002. The strength of this collection is in its expressive range and the inclusion of so many notable YA authors. It's not a title that will keep hearts racing, but it will keep pages turning. Readers will feel a bond with real teens discovering their self-worth within the social sphere of the high school dating scene. (Reproduced, with permission, from *School Library Journal* Copyright © by Reed Business Information A division of Reed Elsevier Inc., June 2002, Vol. 48, Iss. 6, p. 150) (grades 6th–9th)

Wynne-Jones, Tim. *Some of the Kinder Planets.* New York: Orchard, 1995. A delightful collection of stories from homework traumas to alien visits, extraordinary experiences told by a word wizard. (grades 5th–8th)

MULTICULTURAL LITERATURE KNOWS NO BOUNDARIES

This is the dawning of the age of diversity, which makes multicultural literature all the rage. The literary world of differences is vast and expansive. The more titles available, the more complicated the selection process becomes. So how do you select the materials best suited for your programs?

Whittle down the choices to highly recommended titles that coordinate with your school's curriculum. Attend team meetings so that you are able to effectively target themes and issues. Take a close look at the surrounding community and student body and represent their varied cultural, ethnic, and social backgrounds. Then branch out.

The deeper that a novel delves into a character's personal obstacles couched within their unique culture, the greater the likelihood readers will identify with them. Nudge students out of their inner circle to extend beyond themselves. They tend to gravitate toward alter-egos and resist venturing beyond their immediate adolescent concerns. Select stories where teens in different settings, from different ethnic, social, and/or religious backgrounds, are wrestling with coming-of-age turmoil. Fostering family or romantic relationships, fending off unwanted advances, protecting a sibling, developing a bond with an animal—all of these connections translate into any culture. If students can empathize with the characters, they will step into new worlds even if the shoes pinch.

Literature that has the strength of phrase and language to carry an English instructional unit on creative writing is another challenge. Though many novels are set in other countries and cultural environments, not all have the literary clout for the English curriculum. Such a novel should have a plot construction that is energetic and unpredictable. It should display original thinking, a distinct writing style, and imaginative, inspirational, and original vocabulary. Ulti-mately, it should provide themes that have the edginess to push students beyond conventional thinking and to prompt group conversation and debate. Character development should be cohesive, credible, and convincing. Perhaps the most essential element (without it, you'll lose these readers) is that the main character be somebody with whom teens connect. They need to laugh, cry, and be touched by familiar feelings within the unfamiliar environment. Self-righteous characters developed to serve the purpose of delivering a message are transparent and serve a superficial and manipulative marketing intent—the very things we fight.

If you braid the elements of strong characterization, unique and diverse cultural settings, and themes that pique the conscience, you'll have a multicultural collection that students will want to read. They crave to know of kids who break outside the clan, who take risks, who quest for freedom and survive their hard-won independence. They'll identify with characters finding their way through unfamiliar circles. The commonality is that we are all finding our way through unfamiliar cycles of life, no matter our age or culture.

Elsa Marston, commenting on Middle Eastern children's and YA literature has written:

> In these times, when our nation is so entangled in the Arab/Muslim world, Americans urgently need a more accurate and open-minded acquaintance with that part of the global village. Good books for children are an obvious first step.
>
> I'm speaking here particularly of fiction, because I believe it's fiction that has the deepest, most lasting effect on a young person. A good story, appealing to the emotions and offering characters with whom the reader can identify, can help form impressions that a young person carries through life—subliminal attitudes that influence the adult's perception of the world and its peoples.[4]

So is the case with all cultures, and this simply underscores the importance of having a multicultural literature program in place within your school. Developing a quick-fire collection is the librarian's passion. For multicultural literature to infuse the nucleus of the school, provide the material. The only magic is the bibliographic compilations available. There is a rich assortment of these in and of themselves. Hazel Rochman's *Against Borders: Promoting Books for a Multicultural World*[5] is still excellent. *Hearing All the Voices*[6] is an unusual and comprehensive resource, complete with annotated bibliographies organized by theme, literary circle designs, and an open-minded focus beyond multiethnicity. Some North Country Schools (NCS)selections that coordinate with our curriculum and student body are offered below. These should serve only as a guide. Select the titles and read or skim them to get a gut sense of what will jive with, or jar, the comfort zone of your community. For a well rounded representation, have both.

Introduce multicultural material to your faculty at least the spring before they will start a program. Select novels, a novel-in-verse, and several separate short story anthologies. Mark the must-read stories within the collections. Put these offerings into your faculties' hands before they take off for their summer vacation. When you reconvene in the fall, help them to order the titles that they've decided on. Check with your distributors. Because it is a library literature program used within the core curriculum, you should be able to order multiple titles and receive the library price discount. Make it as easy for faculty, and affordable, as possible.

MULTICULTURAL TITLES: AN ANNOTATED BIBLIOGRAPHY

Al-Windawi, Thura. *Thura's Diary: My Life in Wartime Iraq*. New York: Viking, 2004. English translation of the diary of the 19-year-old daughter in a middle-class Shia Muslim family in Baghdad. Thura's experiences living in war through June 2003 put a teen face, voice, and empathy on the struggles of the Iraqi people. (grades 5th–8th)

Buss, Fran Leeper. *Journey of the Sparrows*. New York: Dell, 1991. Salvadoran refugees are smuggled into the United States in crates and try to eke out a living in Chicago. A realistic view of the immigrant experience. (grades 6th–HS)

Crew, Linda. *Children of the River*. New York: Delacorte, 1989. After a harrowing escape from Cambodia to escape the Khmer Rouge army, 17-year-old Sundara is torn between remaining faithful to her own people and assimilating into life, and love, in her high school as a "regular" American teen. (grades 7th–HS)

Gallo, Donald, ed. *First Crossing: Stories about Teen Immigrants*. Cambridge, MA: Candlewick, 2004. Covering a wide range of cultural and economic backgrounds, these stories by eleven well-known authors touch on a variety of teen experiences, with enough attitude and heartfelt angst to speak to young adults everywhere. (Reproduced, with permission, from *School Library Journal* Copyright © by Reed Business Information A division of Reed Elsevier Inc. A. Follos. *School Library Journal*, Oct. 2004, Vol. 50, Iss. 10, p. 164.) (grades 7th–HS)

Gallo, Donald, ed. *Join In: Multiethnic Short Stories by Outstanding Writers for Young Adults*. New York: Delacorte, c1993. Seventeen authors contribute over forty stories and poems featuring teenagers in America from diverse ethnic backgrounds, including Native American, Hispanic American, African American, and Asian American authors. [grades 7th–HS]

Gordon, Sheila. *Waiting for the Rain: A Novel of South Africa*. New York: Bantam, 1989. Chronicles the lives of two South African youths: one black, one white; one with opportunity, one without. Their friendship dissolves in a violent confrontation between student and soldier. (grades 7th–HS)

Mosher, Richard. *Zazoo: A Novel*. New York: Clarion, 2001. From her Vietnamese homeland Zazoo now lives with her adoptive grandfather in France. A beautiful and lyrical novel. A story of love, devotion, and commitment to the elderly that bridges generations and cultures. (Reproduced, with permission, from *School Library Journal* Copyright © by Reed Business Information A division of Reed Elsevier Inc. A. Follos. *School Library Journal*, Nov. 2001, Vol. 47, Iss. 11, p. 162.) (grades 6th–9th)

Rochman, Hazel, and Darlene Z. McCampbell. *Leaving Home: Stories*. New York: HarperCollins, 1998. An international anthology of teens making their way in the world, features stories from fifteen contemporary writers, including: Amy Tan, Toni Morrison, Gary Soto, and Tim Wynne-Jones. (grades 6th–HS)

Staples, Suzanne Fisher. *Shabanu: Daughter of the Wind*. New York: Knopf, 1991. Desert life in Pakistan during the late 1980s, this book offers a view of a young girl's quest for identity in a culture that forbids any gesture or expression of independence by women. Recipient of these awards: 1990 Newbery Honor Book, ALA Notable Book, ALA Best Book for Young Adults. (grades 5th–9th)

Stratton, Allan. *Chanda's Secret*. New York: Annick, 2004. Chandra, a 16-year-old in a small South African town, faces down fear and shame in her efforts to help friends and family members who are dying of AIDS. Sad but real. A young female student who lived part-time in Africa and worried full-time about AIDS confided, "This is my favorite book." (grades 7th–HS)

Watkins, Yoko Kawashima. *So Far from the Bamboo Grove.* New York: Lothrop, Lee & Shepard, 1986. A fictionalized autobiography of an 11-year-old girl who escapes from Korea to Japan with her mother and sister at the end of World War II. (grades 5th–8th)

They say that the world is getting smaller. Mass communication and intercontinental travel are making it so. But when you're trying to gather secular literary material from all over the globe—intent on satisfying and enlightening students within their own tribe—the world feels like a galaxy. You feel piddly and insignificant. How do you keep from becoming intimidated and inundated? Collaborate with your faculty. Use their ideas to help refine the prospects and to zero-in on specific areas. Hate to give up those perfect titles that don't quite fit into the curriculum themes? Plug them into a schoolwide reading program. You'll contribute to launching good titles that have yet to filter through the invisible force field of the teen universe.

NOTES

1. Ed Sullivan, "Fiction or Poetry?" *School Library Journal*, Aug. 2003, p. 44.
2. *Scarecrow Resource Guide Series* (Lanham, MD: Scarecrow Press, 2002).
3. Tim Wynne-Jones, "Short Tempered," *Horn Book Magazine*, May/June 1999, p. 294.
4. Elsa Marston, "A Window in the Wall: Palestinians in Children's Literature," *Horn Book Magazine*, Nov./Dec. 2004, Vol. LXXX, Iss. 6, p. 648.
5. Hazel Rochman, *Against Borders: Promoting Books for a Multicultural World* (Chicago: American Library Association, 1993).
6. Mary Ann Darby and Miki Pryne, *Hearing All the Voices* (Lanham, MD: Scarecrow, 2002).

Chapter 6

COLLECTION AND ADOLESCENT DEVELOPMENT: WHAT *IS* "APPROPRIATE"?

Perhaps the largest professional obstacle you will face in a school library is selecting the right literature for children and young adults. It is a hurdle because selection is so subjective. What is appropriate for some students will not work for others. As an intellectually heterogeneous place, the library safely serves and welcomes all. Yet every competent school librarian knows that questionable material has a purpose and disturbing the status quo is the liberty of literature in a free society. Nonetheless, school librarians must deal with the reality of a diverse audience: age, culture, family beliefs, and development stage. With the profusion of radical young adult (YA) reads on the market, it becomes increasingly difficult to find plain-old feel-good titles. They do exist; they're just not easy to find. Maybe it's a sign of our times, but the majority of contemporary YA titles have a dark side.

Using the delineation of age to place "age-appropriate" material into students' hands is a murky and uncertain practice. A scrawny little 10-year-old boy may look physically immature but intellectually may be a brainiac wrestling with the state of world affairs, or possibly coping with the emotional conflicts of emerging sexuality. Alternately, a tall, striking 14-year-old ingénue may suffer a reading dysfunction and be emotionally immature for her years. Making decisions based solely on age-appropriate guidelines is presumptuous.

With the profusion of issue-oriented YA literature hitting the scene, who should decide what kids are ready to handle? It becomes a matter of professional competence, responsibility, expertise, and yes, common sense. And it lands in your lap. You'll spend long hours reading and considering whether edgy titles will strengthen and broaden your collection, help to illuminate readers about differences, empower them with knowledge, or merely serve to raise a red flag of controversy.

Susan Cooper, director for the Center for International and Cultural Awareness at Wesley College in Dover, DE, has written, "Controversy for the sake of sensationalism is exploitation; the truth within a framework that defines the human experience is not. It is not a question of what is contentious, it truly is a matter of how the material is presented, and most importantly, why. Real life cannot be glossed over, even for the very young. Vehicles for the honest exploration of the journey will enable readers to arm themselves for what may loom ahead."[1]

Our school library serves 9-year-olds through 16-year-olds, a wide spectrum with vastly different intellectual capabilities and physical, emotional, and developmental needs. In the seventeen years that I've been a school librarian I have observed that students read what they are ready for. This is one of the most gratifying and refreshing features of reading in a free society. Readers engage in literature through their personal willingness, intellectual readiness, and emotional preparedness. Due to the cognitive investment that reading demands, an independent reader is not subjected to offensive material as an innocent bystander. If the reader isn't able to understand sophisticated concepts or is disturbed by emotional subject matter, they're able to do a few things: skip over the disturbing section, discuss content with someone who might help them to process the material, block it out (the same way that children do with scary material in fairy tales), or set the book aside.

YA author Chris Crutcher, writing about the things that he would like to take, as well as leave at the door of the new millennium includes:

> our fear of kids reading tough stories; our fear of our children being exposed to things that make them uncomfortable. What I would take with us instead is a new willingness to explore those uncomfortable things with them in an environment that allows us to listen to their responses, and them to listen to ours. Face it; that fear comes mostly from parents, and rightly so. But what parents and teachers alike need to acknowledge is that kids are developmentally programmed to identify our fears—those things we shy away from talking about—and sprint headlong toward them to take a closer look.[2]

And so it bears repeating: Native American tales protected children and fairy tales prepared innocent kids for the monsters in the neighborhood.

A colleague of mine has intervened at times with what she calls preventive medicine. She's taken books out of a 4th-grader's hands and said, "Sorry, maybe when you're in 8th grade." Her rationale is that many of her 4th- and 5th-grade girls tend to "read up", and though they're able to comprehend the vocabulary, they may not be ready for the concepts. An example she gave was a student that checked out *The Sisterhood of the Traveling Pants*. The 4th-grader innocently asked her mother what "virginity" meant, and the mom came back to the school asking why her daughter had such a book.

Personally, I wonder how many children have not heard this word. As far as I'm aware, the Virgin Mary is not an unmentionable figure in most households. When a child asks such a question, it may be time to give him or her the answer. Girls as young as nine years old are menstruating (yes, that's 4th grade), so knowing about their biological development makes good sense. Sexuality and procreation are not dirty concepts unless we make them so.

Libraries are the foundation blocks for all sorts of knowledge for all sorts of people. That's why they exist, and that's why the ALA Code of Ethics states, "We uphold the principles of intellectual freedom and resist all efforts to censor library resources."

In November 2005 Chris Crutcher was honored with the prestigious Celebration of Free Speech and Its Defenders Award. In accepting his award he said:

> I accept this award in the names of all those teachers and librarians who know a story is sometimes better than it ever had a right to be because of the history the

reader brings to the reading, and who honor those readers' histories, defying the censors, bringing those stories into their classrooms and libraries. And for the teachers of teachers in colleges and universities all over the country, who know the desperate times into which our educational system has fallen, because of simple, lazy notions requiring classroom teachers to test their students into comas, who know that if we don't bring the passion of expression back into education, no child will be left behind because nobody's going anywhere.[3]

MAKING CHOICES FOR CHILDREN AND YOUNG ADULTS

When developing your collection you'll have your students' interests at heart while staying aware of your faculty's instructional needs. For the purpose of this chapter, we'll concentrate on developing the fiction and entertainment areas, the most likely areas to be the cause for dissent and discomfort among well-meaning adults.

Some basic considerations in developing a well-balanced collection follow.

- Is the content disturbingly graphic?
- Is the dialogue trendy? If so, the book will become dated.
- Is there an overt theme? Does it overpower the storyline?
- Do the author's ideas stretch beyond the basic theme and plot?
- Is there sensationalism, sex, or bad language for the sake of exploitation?
- Is there resolution?
- Does the story extract empathy from the reader?

And last but not least, the "F-word" and other curses. Are there so many swear words that they overtake and flag more attention than the storyline? Keep in mind that profanities will stand out glaringly when read aloud. They also shout when taken out of context. If you've read the novel silently and profanity has been swallowed-up and has gone unnoticed within the content, that's how you should judge the book. If you are overtly aware of profanity, there may be an editorial problem, making it a questionable purchase for a middle school collection. Yet it may be quite suitable for a high school library. As with all literature, you really need to consider the writing, the message, and whether the offensive language is drawing more attention than the intent of the story.

COMMONSENSE COLLECTING

Once you determine the guidelines for developing your collection, all that is left is making the purchases. Finding your way to the best books is not difficult if you have access to the best review journals. You are entitled to these indispensable professional resources. Budget your way clear to subscribe to at least two. There are many dependable ones, and they offer numerous articles that pertain to your daily concerns. Use several to gain a balanced picture on individual titles. Have a highlighter and Post-It note flags ready when you go through the journals. If you're borrowing them through the school library interlibrary loan system, have a pen and paper to jot down notes and titles. Note a student or staff member's name that might particularly enjoy the book. Otherwise, by the time the order arrives (sometimes months after you've begun a title list) you may have forgotten why, or for whom, the book was ordered.

Read reviews carefully, but unless a single author grabs your attention, do not attempt to read every review. Hit all the starred reviews, and focus on new titles from your favorite authors. Collect journals for a few months, accumulating them well after you've skimmed the starred reviews and articles. Then take a few evenings, or a weekend morning with a cup of coffee, to sort through them again to refine the list that you'll order. Here are just some of the many book review journals that will help with this process:

School Library Journal, P.O. Box 16388, North Hollywood, CA 91615, published monthly, subscription: $124

The Horn Book, 56 Roland St., Suite 200, Boston, MA 02129, published six times a year, subscription: $49

Voice of Youth Advocates, VOYA, Scarecrow Press, 4501 Forbes Blvd., Suite 200, Lanham, MD 20706, published 6 times a year, subscription: $35

Booklist, P.O. Box 607, Mt. Morris, IL 61054-7564, published 22 times a year, subscription: $89.95

Library Media Connection, LMC, 480 E. Wilson Bridge Rd., Suite L, Worthington, OH 43085, published 7 times during the school year, subscription: $69

BOOK REVIEWING WILL STRENGTHEN YOUR COLLECTION

If your school library system participates in a book review cooperative with publishers, get involved. Reviewing new books is an invaluable discipline that will benefit your school population. You will need to wade through some ho-hum titles, but in doing so, you'll have a grasp on what's hit the market and you may discover some "sleeper" titles that would never claim your attention in the review journals. I have reviewed a ton of nondescript and unimpressive titles to which I've had lukewarm reactions. A year later a teacher will be looking for the exact subject, setting, or time period in which the story takes place. It may be the only book in our collection that fits the need. Uncanny but true. You can't discredit the serendipitous benefits of reviewing.

Here's a case in point: When I reviewed Louis Sachar's book *Holes*, I knew that it would be perfect for my Reader's Workshop class (see Reader's Workshop, Chapter 8). It would be a solid year before *Holes* garnered the Newbery. When I received *Holes*, I knew a gift had landed in my lap. I'm not always so lucky to receive such a sure-thing novel. The thing is, if you don't invest time reviewing and culling through the crop, you won't taste the fruit. *Holes* happened for my students years before the movie came out. That's the edge I want.

You may want to try reviewing for some of the professional journals. They will ask you to submit a sample of your work, so gain some experience before jumping in. Many professional magazines are looking for good reviewers who work with students. You'll find yourself over run with mediocre titles but will also get a sneak preview of what is available.

Consider book reviewing an elemental part of your continuing education. It is a constant challenge to find the time to read these books, and then invest the additional time to summarize them. Nonetheless, it is an invaluable investment from a professional perspective. It puts you in the best position to know what's available, and it enables you to broadcast the information to faculty members. The problem with reviewing is that your "adult" reading time will be nonexistent. I'm frequently put in the embarrassing situation with my friends asking, "Have you read..." to which I must respond, "Is it a children's book?" The exception is when Anne Lamott has a new title. I identify with her obsessions and hold tight to the belief that she's nuttier than I am—yet her writing is measured, natural, and brilliantly composed. Her books offer me personal reprieve and make me laugh. The truth is, sometimes I could kill to have the time to read an adult novel. I'm embarrassed to admit that I've still not read the *DiVinci Code*, for example. However, I'm pressed to keep up with the newest titles and literary trends in the children's and YA market. I'm trapped. Here's a well-kept professional secret: Being a school librarian is a 12-month commitment, with 10 months allotted to teaching students and 12 months in search of the best books for them.

Reviewing gives me the added bonus of always having fresh material for classes. Because of the many titles I review, when I introduce a book to my students I'm spared from the annoying chirp, "I've already read it." My class members gain a sneak preview before other students. I'm sure to let them know this, and they recognize the advantage and enjoy the privilege. In fact, they love it. I enlist their help to give me the thumbs-up or thumbs-down response. If I love a title to which they have a bored response, I want to know why. In order to do a good job representing the best titles for the children and YA audience, include students in the action. An adult's critique is only the tip of the assessment: The students are the real test.

I also pass along my review material to my faculty. Recently an English teacher was having an impossible time coming up with something new and fresh to introduce to his 8th-grade students. I was quick to share *Where We Are What We See*, the 2005 Scholastic/Push Cart best-of-the-best teen collection of prose, poetry, short stories, and fine art that David Levithan edited. This teacher was so appreciative that he now comes in several times a week to let me know how the class is going, and we're collaborating on a short story mini-unit for next semester.

Reviewing also calls your attention to all manner of authors, editors, and publishers, many of whom escape notice through the review journals.

If you offer to review, request an age group, theme, and/or genre preference, for example: animal stories, YA fantasy, story collections, poetry, etc. Pinpoint subjects that your curriculum will benefit from. You'll want the time you're investing to be well applied toward your, and your faculty's, instructional areas.

CONFERENCE CONFISCATIONS

If you want to collect the newest, hottest, most likely to be promoted and publicized titles, then attend conferences. (There are other good reasons to attend conferences, but for the purpose of this chapter, we'll stick to the freebies.) You'll meet the authors, be able to purchase their books, and often have those books autographed. Even better, you'll be loaded-down with free "advance reader's copies" of new titles. We selected our 9th-grade English book *Secrets in the Fire* (Toronto: Annick, 2003) from previewing a promotional copy. The

English teacher was delighted to introduce a new multicultural title that none of the students had heard of.

If you're fortunate enough to attend the annual American Library Association (ALA) conference, go prepared to take the time to collect and ship books home. Publishers regale librarians with their new titles, generously heaping them into willing arms. If you are able to stay until the end, you'll reap duplicate copies simply because the publishers don't want to cart them away. Pass along these copies to your faculty. They'll appreciate being alerted to new titles that are applicable to their teaching needs. In addition to providing a preview of what's on tap in the coming months, these titles are great reading incentive awards.

COLLECTING FOR THE GENERAL WELFARE

My book budget and shelf space are limited, so I make a tough call on series titles. It's been my experience that series are readily available at bookstores and inevitably are purchased by my students. Having said that, it is important to have the heavily requested titles available in order to serve students equally. Think about creative options, like acquiring Harry Potter titles through a student's family's donation. Many families are delighted to pass along their literary cast-offs. (Gently remind them that you hold the right to cast off the cast-offs.)

Another drawback to series titles is that, because of their trendiness, they tend to have a limited circulation life. The worst part about series titles is that students enter school looking for the third, or perhaps the seventh, title in a series that nobody has ever asked for before. If students haven't requested these titles prior to this point, it's not practical to suddenly buy one book out of sequence. You certainly won't want to invest in the entire series. This is a perfect time to teach students about the benefits of interlibrary loan. A student who is excited about getting the next book in a series will see the immediate advantage of interlibrary loan and will pay attention to the instruction.

It *is* important to keep the collection fresh and popular—but not at short-term expense lacking long-range significance. Your goal is to develop a collection that's vital to the age you serve and acquire literature that will endure the test of time.

You'll want to collect material that is kid-friendly, entertaining, and exciting. The manga graphic novels are a must, but you don't need them all. I caution you to give them a quick once-over before displaying them. In this new and burgeoning market you can't rely on the reviews or advertisements to paint the full picture. I've been surprised, more than once, to find an abundance of naked females in less-than-demure poses. One of my students complained about being offended by graphic language and illustrations that had escaped my attention. I thought he was overreacting and I brought the book home for a more scrutinizing look. Sure enough, it opened immediately to the well-worn pages revealing balloon-encapsulated profanity and females in sexually suggestive situations. I've yet to find naked males, but that's another tangent. There are plenty of graphic novels that aren't overtly sexually explicit, and therefore very appropriate for school libraries. There are also many fun and gamelike books that are produced to captivate and entertain: *Eye-Spy*, *Guinness Book of Records*, *Where's Waldo*, and *Magic Eye* all offer a visual element to pull students in for their entertainment value. Listen to your students' requests and honor them. I do lots of bartering.

I may offer to order an unusual title for a student if he or she is willing to read one—or two—books that I suggest.

DON'T JUDGE A MAGAZINE BY ITS COVER

An appealing magazine collection will tempt students and staff members into the library. The only time you may see these patrons is when the new *Sports Illustrated*, *Rolling Stone*, *Newsweek*, *Snowboarding*, or *Teen People* arrives. If you want to pull in all kinds of readers, then your magazine collection must reflect your audience's tastes, not yours.

Depend upon professional resources to help you develop a varied collection. Julie Bartel's comprehensive "The Good, the Bad and the Edgy" in the July 2005 issue of *School Library Journal* comes complete with annotations and age-appropriate guidelines. Watching how often the magazines are being used (or stolen) also helps you determine what is in highest demand. I threaten my students that I won't reorder *Teen People* because it's always being filched. Of course I will, because it is so obviously—if corruptly—coveted. But I do try to dissuade the culprit by using community guilt tactics. My threat of not reordering gets out into the teen grapevine and peer pressure is an effective deterrent.

Magazines rely on eye-catching covers. Even *Outside* magazine, devoted to outdoor activities, camping, travel, climbing, biking, and other popular sporting activities is known for tantalizing covers that capture attention. In the April 2005 issue, a sepia-toned photo of an artfully posed nude woman graced the cover of *Outside*. Inside was a feature article on women rock climbers with a photo accompaniment—a clever ruse to lure readers to sample an article about the strengths and passion of women rock climbers. My point here is that even though magazine cover art and commercial advertising ploys that support the journal may use exploitive techniques, it remains your responsibility to evaluate the magazine's content. Make an intelligent judgment call based on your audience's—not your own—interest and the magazine's content—not its cover.

BEST INTENTIONS BUILD SOLID COLLECTIONS

The librarian's best intentions will be unable to comb out every title that will pass adult scrutiny. If your collection provides material for a mix of personalities, a range of intelligences, and a diverse population, then you are sure to please many and offend some. This assures that your collection is as eclectic and interesting as its audience.

The most effective way to get the right books into your students' hands is to know your students. Make rapport with students a priority in your daily contacts. Students will not always know what they need to read, but they need to know that they are welcome to read anything. They should not feel inhibited or embarrassed by their choices. Don't protect students from their own curiosity: The library is the place to go for answers. Your 4th-grade student is not going to pluck Sylvia Plath's *The Bell Jar* (New York: Harper Row, 1971) or Melvin Burgess's *Smack* (New York: Henry Holt, 1996) off the shelf any more than you will place it into their hands. Like harrowing fairy tales that children absorb or block out, depending on their emotional temperament, teens will read what they're ready for. Conversely, don't subject students to material that is overtly heavy with subject matter that they don't care to explore. While some readers will gravitate toward angst, tumult, and exploitation, others will want the recreational escape of fantasy, romance, or historical fiction. A good collection will have it all.

Invest plenty of time in assessing literature that will most effectively serve your community. Stay nonjudgmental and objective. Fighting censorship does not mean forsaking common sense. A school library will honor students' emotional development as well as their academic needs. As the professional adult, you need to make decisions with a trained and confident eye. Be willing to defend your collection for the benefit of your students' intellectual welfare, expressive freedom, and literary growth. As a former ALA president, Carol Brey-Casiano has said, "Not every book is right for every person, but providing a wide range of reading choices is vital for learning, exploration and imagination. The abilities to read, speak, think and express ourselves freely are core American values."[4]

NOTES

1. Susan Cooper, "Only the Rarest Kind of Best—One View of Literary Criticism," *Children and Libraries*, Summer/Fall 2005, pp. 14–17.
2. Chris Crutcher, "R*E*S*P*E*C*T: For Kids, Adolescence, for Story," *Voices from the Middle*, Dec. 1999, Vol. 7, Iss. 2, p. 17.
3. Chris Crutcher, Celebration of Free Speech and Its Defenders Award, Acceptance Speech, National Coalition Against Censorship, Rubin Museum of Art, November 7, 2005, New York, NY.
4. ALA Banned Book Week 2005 (http://www.ala.org/ala/oif/bannedbooksweek/challengedbanned/challengedbanned.htm).

REFERENCES

Follos, Alison. Summer/Fall 2005. "Jack Gantos on Writing: Digging Up Creative Juices from Restaurants to Graveyards." *Children & Libraries*. Vol. 3, Iss. 2, 42–44.
Krashen, Stephen D. *The Power of Reading*. Westport, CT: Libraries Unlimited, 2004. 137.

Part III

<u>PROGRAMS</u>

Chapter 7

TITLE TREKKING: A READING INCENTIVE PROGRAM

A PEAK READING EXPERIENCE

Ever become frustrated because the great "complete" National Geographic CD collection won't run on the new computers, the ProQuest renewal subscription won't accept the old password, and when you unplugged the printer—because it doesn't have an "on/off" switch—you bash your head (yet again) on the desk while coming up from under a dusty tangle of wires trying to locate the power reset? What ever happened to the reason you became a librarian in the first place—what about the books?

At our small school faculty members are encouraged to think outside the box and make instruction meaningful and motivational for our students. Having creative liberty can serve as a blessing and a curse—big ideas generate more work. I've been encouraged to promote our schoolwide reading incentive program, and despite the extra work, I'm delighted. Because in my mind, if I were a librarian surrounded by books without readers, what would be the point?

TREKKING THE PEAKS

Sixteen years ago we began to think about a schoolwide reading program for middle and upper school students: A reading program that would serve a variety of needs without having to be annually revised and reintroduced, that would be "owned" by the school community and not "belong" to the library. We wanted a reading program to tempt the most reluctant readers and challenge the most discriminating. What began as a way to wedge good books into kids' hands is now part of the distinction that contributes to North Country School's eclectic educational style. We call our reading program Title Trekking. This is why:

Once upon a time in the heart of the Adirondacks, there were high peaks silently challenging men and women to hike them, because, well, they were there. As years went by, hikers answered the call to best the peaks—not merely one, or two, but all forty-six of the high peaks with elevations over 4,000 feet. It became a feat to which climbers continue to aspire. Publicly, these climbers are regaled as "Adirondack 46'ers." Rugged hikers devote many years of outdoor commitment to fulfilling this goal. For some it's a long pursuit, culminating in a carefully planned milestone moment at the peak of their 46th climb: birthday celebrations, marriage proposals, even weddings are often timed to coincide with the accomplishment of the goal. For others the treks become a lifelong climbing habit: a goal completed, only to begin again. The type-A goal-oriented may decide to tackle the 46'ers during the seasons, becoming Fall 46'ers, Winter 46'ers, Spring 46'ers, and Summer 46'ers—some all four. It's a trek that keeps on going. I'm not much on hiking, but I must say, I'm indebted to the symbolism that it has given to our reading program. We dubbed it Title Trekking for the obvious metaphorical connection.

TITLE TREKKING

Our whole-school reading incentive program links forty-six mountain peaks with forty-six books. The geographical landscape, the physical endurance, the stamina built-up from hiking, are all synonymous with the intellectual gains acquired through reading. It's brain exercise. Readers begin, as they would with climbing mountains, where they feel comfortable and capable. The varied elevations provide age-appropriate guidelines and reading challenge suggestions. Lower elevations suggest easier reading, whereas the highest peaks represent YA titles or adult titles suitable for older students.

Organized within this 46'er framework is a list compiled of highly readable titles. There isn't any specific delineation between grades, allowing students the choice and flexibility of reading titles that pique their interest. Matching the titles to mountains provides a visible measurement of each student's progress. A record of every title that a student scales is displayed in the library and in the English classrooms.

The real gem of this program is that it flows from school year through summer, 4th grade through graduation, year after year, encouraging students to read continually and have reading become a natural leisure pastime. Much like the love for mountain climbing has developed in rugged Adirondack 46'ers, we strive to instill the same intrinsic, lifelong passion in our readers.

JIVING WITH THE CURRICULUM

We've also taken collaborative steps to meet the English department's needs. Title Trekking encourages students to read beyond the classroom, while integrating literature into the classroom. It doesn't compete or clash with the curriculum; it works in tandem with it. Curriculum themes are certainly considered when compiling the title lists, but "highly readable" literature drives it.

To have this collaboration work for you, request time during staff meetings to booktalk with your faculty. Chat up material that will be particularly relevant to their curriculum themes. In exchange for your input, faculty members will reciprocate, which helps you to tie the reading program to their classes. Professional regard, respect, and communication help to strengthen mutual academic intent. Remaining a stand-alone library program reduces the program's popularity and blocks community acceptance.

In order to best align the library's collection with the English department's needs, stay attuned to curriculum transitions. Know what has transpired in past years and what's in the forecast. When a faculty member plans a unit on the Harlem Renaissance, start combing the market and identifying material to include on the reading list. Select complementary titles that aren't necessarily part of the class reading requirement but will bolster the interest level. This produces a strong literary immersion in theme and content without the pressure of a classroom assignment. The point is to complement, not impose or usurp, the English curriculum. Develop collective themes in different literary genres and formats:

• Short story collections
• Young adult (YA) anthologies
• Fairy tales
• Mythology
• Historical fiction
• Medieval fiction
• Adventure novels
• Survival tales
• Novels-in-verse
• Biographies
• Author autobiographies

The thematic and subject areas are vast, and it's easy to tailor them to the faculty's needs. Keep these lists in an easy-access bibliography binder next to the students' Title Trek journals. They'll become an indispensable resource for staff when generating ideas.

TREKKING TACKLES MULTIPLE TASKS

The residual effects of a reading incentive program will be absorbed throughout the school. It will become a natural part of the academic program and eventually enlist faculty ownership. If implemented in logical steps, with consideration for the instructional program, the school calendar, and sensitivity toward your students' reading inclinations, the program will be used for years.

The following ideas describe needs that a reading program fills:

1. Foremost, reading incentive programs are a proactive means to introduce masses of good books to busy kids. A lot of top-notch titles are being missed by the very virtue of students' fast physical growth and their jet-paced lifestyle, and quite simply, because they aren't introduced to the goods in a systematic and timely manner.

2. The program generates a list, overarching grade levels to accommodate readers' interests and intellects, as opposed to linking with the arbitrary "age-appropriate" formula. It also provides a summer reading list of contemporary titles. The list therefore stays usable and current because it is updated twice a year.

3. Staff and students rely on these reading suggestions, trusting them to be interesting, highly readable, and contemporary children's and YA literature. Your reading recommendations should go beyond the award winners, beyond the overused classics, and include the new and best "good reads" that have the potential to propel YA literature into a thriving market.

4. Faculty members will become aware of the mass of children's and YA titles that will shore-up their classes. Many teachers are still relying on *Mrs. Frisby and the Rats of NIMH* (New York: Atheneum, 1971) or *Julie of the Wolves* (New York: Harper & Row, 1972). These are great books, but while depending on "old favorites," too many new titles sink into shelved obscurity before reaching an audience.

5. New books need a quick delivery or they'll quickly become old titles—children just grow up too fast. A Title Trek reading list strives to include recently published titles culled from professional reviews that librarians are privy to, but the general public is not. When you handpick titles for your school community, tailoring them to specific students, you guarantee a following.

6. Journaling. Once students have read a book, they write a brief, descriptive summary of the book in their own words. They are to consider their journal a literary diary and note distinctive elements of the literature that they'll want to remember ten years from now. The entry is not the dreaded book report. Students and staff take a moment from their fast-paced day to reflect upon literature by writing about it. A Title Trek journal provides an avenue for readers to summarize the story, consider their empathetic reactions to the characters, and describe their personal assessment of the story. If several students enter a negative comment on a title, I'll remove the book from our list. The purpose of "reading incentive" is to keep kids reading. This won't happen if they don't like the books (see "Tracking Those Treks" below, and Reader's Workshop and Journaling, Chapter 9).

7. In exchange for their journal entries, readers receive a human response, a dialogue of shared impressions about the books they are reading and reactions to their reading comprehension. There's nothing electronically generated, accelerated, or automated— just an old-fashioned personal response from a person: me.

8. Title Trekking's success is that it's designed as a schoolwide program, ongoing throughout a student's attendance. Students begin in 4th grade, continue reading through the summers, accumulate titles each year, and keep Trekking through 9th grade graduation. Theoretically, by the time they're in high school reading is a pleasurable part of their daily routine.

Title Trekking Traits:

- Title Trekking is not easy. It's challenging and, for many students, that's its appeal.
- It has a competitive edge.
- Students set their own goals.
- Their progress is visibly displayed in the library and in the classroom.
- Students read books that are selected just for them by a librarian familiar with their interests, reading tastes, and ability.
- Students are encouraged to stretch their reading desires and branch into other genres.

These strategies won't work overnight: They take planning and slow and careful implementation. The following ideas will help get you started.

SIMPLE, SMART, AND SMARMY TOO

First, find a gimmick. Use any environmental, geographical, or regional symbol that works: lakes, rivers, sports teams, streets and avenues, or neighborhood districts. Try to use something that will work conceptually with your school's motto, location, or claim to fame.

Next, create a reading list that will serve several purposes, that is: satisfying the English department's summer recommendations; quick picks for students on the run between classes; a mix of titles that will appeal to a mix of different tastes; suggestions for staff eager to become knowledgeable about children's and YA titles; and a compilation that reflects recently released and well-received titles.

This list should be smart and alluring. Use smarmy marketing techniques that get attention. Think romance and adventure, humor and horror. Shake off the sensible shoes and take out the strappy heels. Use titles that are likely to whet their appetite, make adults wince, and keep students coming back for more. Remember, the stuff that makes us uncomfortable, they love. Books like *The Silver Kiss* by Annette Curtis Clause (New York: Delacorte, 1990), Melvin Burgess's *Smack* (New York: Henry Holt, 1998), *The China Garden* by Liz Berry (New York: Farrar, Straus and Giroux, 1996), and *Go Ask Alice* (Englewood Cliffs, NJ: Prentice-Hall, 1971) will be devoured. In between these titles, place irresistible literature that they'll enjoy and you'll gladly recommend: Jerry Spinelli's *Loser* (New York: Joanna Cotler, 2002) and *Maniac Magee* (Boston: Little, Brown, 1990), Walter Dean Myers's *Monster* (New York: HarperCollins, 1999), Jennifer Donnelly's *A Northern Light* (San Diego: Harcourt, 2003), Angela Johnson's *First Part Last* (New York: Simon & Schuster, 2003), and David Levinthan's, *Realm of Possibilities* (New York: Random House, 2004).

Develop a reading list that is fresh, fun, and feisty. Use a basic database format that stays constant but makes it simple to insert revisions as new titles emerge (view the North Country School [NCS] Title Trek database list online at http://nct.org/library).

TEMPTING TREKKERS

The most obvious but overlooked glitch in reading incentive programs is a failure to keep newly published titles out there for voracious readers: the students who have "read everything," and who feel that the school library has nothing to offer that they haven't already read, or, would ever want to read. Change their disdain into excitement by keeping your collection fresh, with many new titles that will tempt them. Instead of acting bored, they'll respond, "Oh, I love this author! I didn't know they had something new!"

Title Trekking is an independent, goal-oriented program that is fueled by peer interest. I can organize, publicize, and shout all about it, but if kids aren't "into it" I may as well forget about it. More students Trek each year, and the fact that the program is no longer a novelty helps teens accept it. Achieving the status of becoming a literary 46'er is very difficult. Over the past sixteen years we've only had fourteen students, and a few teachers, make it. This challenge gives the program distinction and offers a competitive, status-infused nudge that some students need.

The Title Trek list is revamped during the winter and summer. Past lists are kept for referral, and students may always select titles from any of the numerous lists that have gone before. For your program, keep lists in plastic sheet protectors and insert them in a binder. Shelve them next to the student and staff Title Trek journals for ready access. Develop new lists with different slants.

Though Title Trekking is an independent venture, I do try to provide some tantalizing motivation. I solicit awards from our downtown shops—a gift certificate to the local bookstore, an ice cream, a pencil. Even if the award is little and silly, students love the attention. At the end of the school year I host a party at my house. A student's ticket in is a journal with the number of Treks entered for the school year (Sept.–May), equivalent to their grade level: every 4th-grader who has Trekked four books, every 5th-grader who has Trekked five books, and so on. Staff members who have been Title Trekking are also invited.

TITLE TREKKING AND JOURNALING

A fundamental aspect of the Title Trek program is reflecting upon and providing a written summary of the book in a journal. The journal is a simple marbled covered composition book that is shelved in a central location in the library. A yellow piece of tape serves as a spine label, and adding a number with a Sharpie pen keeps journals shelved in numerical order. The journals may travel to the classroom or home if a student can't find the time to enter their Trek during the day in the library. We encourage students to keep their journals in the library because the journal also serves as their "reader's response journal" for their Reader's Workshop class (see Reader's Workshop and Journaling, Chapter 9).

The journal entries are nonthreatening free-writes: Spelling doesn't matter, though legibility is a necessity. Conceivably, the journal might collect four to five years of a student's writing and literary interpretations. It can contribute to self-measurement of a student's long-term reading comprehension and intellectual growth.

Students uniformly agree that the process of writing about the book they've read is the hardest part of Title Trekking. When I ask why they like Accelerated Reader (a computer-generated program through which students check off answers to books that they've read), their response is, "It's easy!" Title Trekking is not. Even faculty members have difficulty finding the time to write down their thoughts in a journal. However, they are the first to agree that doing so is the most important element of the program for several reasons: It slows down and gives credence to an intellectual process, it creates an indelible personal reflection of the literature, and it provides an annotation to which they may refer back as a teaching resource.

Literature is written to be carefully absorbed. It's a private conversation between an author and a reader. When the reader takes time to consider the work, they give it contemplative attention. We are a gobbling culture. Generally, literature is not created for the speed-reader. The act of slowing down, reflecting, and writing about books feels just *too* time consuming. Yet, it stimulates intellectual activity and fosters literature appreciation.

The Title Trek reading program is exciting, challenging, and successful, but it is not easy, particularly for the librarian. After you have spent oodles of time selecting just the right books for your audience, you must entice, beg, cajole, and/or bribe students to read them, and finally, you must fight the good fight to get students to enter a written summary about the books. They'll doubt the merit of such a "waste of time," and you'll need to explain and convince them that it's worth their energy.

Remember becoming a librarian only to discover it had little to do with getting kids to read? Now readers keep coming back with more and more journal entries for me to read because they enjoy the personal written responses to their thoughts. Title Trekking is based upon sharing and reciprocating an inner passion for literature within a culture that is on a downward slide of ever knowing the pleasure of reading. Your investment is well worth it.

It *is* more work, but it is gratifying work. Having meaningful, personal written exchanges about the current literature that my students and staff are reacting to is professionally stimulating, eye-opening, and integral to my connection with the community. Learning what students are "into" helps me avoid relying on adult assumptions. All the professional review journals can't tell me what kids like as well as kids can. I don't mean to imply that because children love candy, they should live on a diet of sugar. It's more like, when a child is raised on sugar, you introduce them to a feast of attractive alternatives, a smorgasbord to tempt the finicky and satisfy the hungry—a well-balanced selection of books that will whet their literary appetite and nourish their intellect.

Students begin Title Trekking as early as 4th grade, using the same journal throughout their years in middle school. They may fill their first journal and start a second one. Their journal number stays the same. Students become very attached to their journal number in a similar way that student-athletes become attached to their jersey number. There's something tangible when students are able to look back upon reactions to books that they read in 4th grade (maybe it was *Tales of a Fourth Grade Nothing*, *Holes*, or *Because of Winn-Dixie*), and then five years later, as a 9th grader, they have made the jump to more sophisticated titles like Stephen Chbosky's *The Perks of Being a Wallflower* (New York: Pocket Books, 1999), or M.T. Anderson's *Feed* (Cambridge, MA: Candlewick, 2002). From their penmanship to their intellectual and emotional perspectives, these are personal changes that students can measure. By concisely expressing these stories in their own words, they preserve them.

JOURNAL QUESTIONS AND THE GAMES STUDENTS PLAY

Your input need not be lengthy, but a question or two will help readers to clarify their personal reflections. If, once you've read their journal entry, you feel that a student has really missed the meaning of a book, give them some guidance. It doesn't matter what genre you're assessing; it's not difficult to come up with a few open-ended questions. For instance:

- Journeys: Physical and/or emotional—were there any?
- Good vs. evil?
- Quests: Was there one? Was it successful? Why?
- Heroes: Were there any? What makes a hero?
- Did you identify with the main character? If so, why? If not, why?
- Is there a dominant theme to the story? What is it?
- Is there a secondary subtle theme? What is it?

THE JOURNAL ENTRY

Once you get your students writing in their journals, the darker side emerges. Believe it or not, you'll have to limit student and staff entries to two handwritten pages. This helps them to consolidate their thoughts and become disciplined and succinct in their compositions. But students resist all limits—even those that curtail their writing! They will try to write in the tiniest penmanship on the face of the earth and fill two pages with writing that you'll need a magnifying glass to see (and if it were written in a normal size, would cover three to four pages). They think they're pretty funny. Strange as it may seem, this is how you stay personally connected with your students—if sometimes aggravatingly so. The good part is learning that they loved the book and they're eager to write so much about it. Refining is part of the learning process, and because I like to have the last laugh, I'll tease, "Hey, when I have a free weekend, or maybe a month, I'll read your book-length Trek." Two can play these games.

Students will cluster around your desk between every class plaintively wailing, "Have you read my Title Trek yet?" Counter back, "It took you how long to turn in your Title Trek? And you're pestering me to read it right now? Do you think that I have nothing better to do? Can you see how many other journals are on my desk to read—*ahead* of yours I might add?!" In other words, let them suffer your inattention and wait. It's a ruse on your part, but it works like a charm. Your feigned disinterest throws them for a loop. The more it seems like you don't care, the more they do. The more they think they can torment you, the more they will. It's that perverse relationship of teen versus teacher.

The lack-of-attention game may not be quite as fun to play with your faculty. Adults have a stuffy sense of humor and tend to be overachievers. Some staff will stop in the library with a thinly disguised desire to "chat." You'll see them peering past you, checking out your desk, silently judging ("My journal's still on her desk!! What the hell does she do all day?!"). Maybe I'm being paranoid. Nonetheless, it makes me testy. Once they leave, in my quiet, retaliatory way, I place their journal at the bottom of the pile.

Fitting in your written response to this reading program may mean bringing journals home for an evening or two. I've carried them on plane rides to conferences. Model yourself after dedicated English and humanities teachers, lugging those tests and essays home for the weekend. Your personal investment makes a reading incentive program successful.

READERS READ—SO WHAT'S THE FUSS?

Unlike students that are involved in athletics, middle and high school "readers" receive few (if any) public accolades. It's an interesting dichotomy that educators bemoan the plummeting reading test scores, yet deliver scant attention toward those who quietly excel in this area. What about those students who tuck themselves away in a corner trying to maintain their invisibility? They're in a private world. These are students who are being intellectually teleported to places unknown to educators—unmeasured, overlooked, and therefore, invalidated. Do we really wonder why students don't aspire to be readers? Where's the acceptance, excitement, public approval rating? Where's the interest?

These same students may hide in romance or fantasy titles, oblivious to the wealth of other intriguing literature that abounds in the library. Skeptics may scoff, "These students already read. Why fuss over getting them to read more?" My response is that in their cloak of impenetrability they achieve escape, but their passion is isolated and they miss great avenues of possibility. Title Trekking offers these students other genres to explore and introduces them to different authors.

A student athlete is fidgety and unable to concentrate in the classroom, but may be the M.V.P. of the basketball team or a hopeful track star. Their energy is harnessed, focused, trained, and heralded. A confident spirit is fostered in them so that they'll push themselves to achieve more. They are given extra support in their academic struggles while continuing to receive glory for their athletic abilities. This is an accepted and promoted attitude in most schools.

Why isn't this same attention and encouragement applied toward a student reader, helping them to feel good about their intellectual pursuits and aspirations? Why aren't readers cheered and celebrated to popularize the act of reading? Title Trekking participation defines a "reader" as something other than the derogatory image of a wallflower stuck with his or her nose in a book. It applauds intellectual aptitude and celebrates literary interest. Title Trekking offers readers a goal that earns public acclaim. Through the written element of Title Trekking, an avid reader may become more invested in their writing skills, honing and developing their talents to new levels of mastery. Most important, it breeds confidence and self-esteem from their notable literary successes. It's not "American Idol," but it helps a bookworm metamorphose into a celebrity within the crowd.

Reading does not have to be boring, nerdy, or unpopular. In today's competitive world, the quiet titles resting upon the shelves need a dynamic edge to win a following. For the student reader, a reading incentive program shines a light of pride on their inclinations and drums up participation from the crowd. As with athletes, encouraging and supporting our blossoming intellectuals develops bright, confident leaders and encourages new members to join the team.

GETTING STUDENTS TO TREK

The first trek is the hardest. Some years the program runs smoothly on its own momentum; other times it needs a shot in the arm. Use your creative ingenuity to rev it up. Go for material rewards, treats, and high public visibility. The first two are sure things; the third is on a case-by-case situation.

Carry on over every student's Title Trekking accomplishments. Presentations should be awarded during a very public moment like school council or all-school assembly. Recognition should be given the same pomp and flourish that the coach gives to sporting awards. The public acknowledgement promotes reading interest and entices participation.

Not every too-cool teen—especially the painfully shy ones—likes public accolades. Stay sensitive to individual students so you don't sabotage good intentions. It's all in the delivery style. On occasion, quietly bestowing an award may gently lure a shy student into becoming a proud outward participant. I have one student who is my "secret Title Trekker." He and I know the deal, and every other student in the school is dying to know who it is. In this secret way, he's having fun and receiving quiet acknowledgement.

The sillier the awards, the more desirable they become. Conferences are the best source for scavenging for awards. Roaming through the vendor tents at the National Book Festival in Washington, DC, I pilfered through the freebees under the U.S. states tent. Free pencils had state names imprinted on them and often included notable authors from that state. When publicly awarding that first

pencil, I misplaced my glasses and couldn't read the small print. Turning to a
student for assistance, he bellowed out the state with swaggering pride (he
wasn't even from that state!). Because of that silliness, students are eager to
receive a pencil. It's those quirky little moments that you run with. From many
students recording one Title Trek, and receiving a pencil, to a few becoming a
Literary Adirondack 46'er, the point is: Kids are reading.

IT'S ALL ABOUT THE AWARDS

Students believe that material awards are the pleasure that they're after. They
demand, "What do I get if I do ten Title Treks?" My sing-song response, "Oh my,
you get to have read ten wonderful books!" is not what they want to hear. They
chide, "Yeah, right." So then I lure them with the material goods. Of course the
reality is, the stories that they read today are the lasting rewards—they just don't
know that yet.
Here's what gets the greedy-guts participating:

- 5 Title Treks (TT): a toy animal—pig, moose, chicken, etc. (For us, it's the farm school
  and Adirondack wilderness connection.) If I could find a pencil with a pink pig eraser,
  the percentage of schoolwide Trekkers would boom.
- 10 TT: a funky-colored monogrammed notepad
- 20 TT: a $10 gift certificate to the local bookstore
- 25 TT: a gift certificate for a quarter-pound of chocolate from our local candy shop
- 30 TT: an ice cream sundae from the local ice cream shop
- 40 TT: a baseball cap monogrammed with the student's name, the Title Trek program,
  and the year
- 46 TT: in keeping with our mountain theme, a regional Eastern Mountain Sports store
  donates a backpack with the student's initials monogrammed on it. I fill it with books
  and assorted goodies—including their tattered worn journal filled with forty-six
  annotations; four to five years' worth of entries!

When a student or staff becomes an Adirondack Literary 46'er, his or her name
is engraved on a plaque that hangs outside of the library for all eternity. It applauds
those who have gone before and beckons to those yet to join. Getting to this point is
a monumental accomplishment, one achieved by only thirteen students and three
faculty members over the past sixteen years. The high caliber of difficulty elevates
the Trekker to a distinction held by few, honored by many—attainable but not
easy. The quest remains challenging yet conquerable, and the final ascent is
powerful. Students and staff encourage one another heartily as they near the end
of their Trekking experiences. For me, the best reward is the aftermath, when a
student previously on the fence comes into the library and requests a book to Title
Trek. They've been inspired by those who've taken on the challenge.
The year-end party at my house is also used to generate classroom investment
and is realistically attainable by all students. It's deliberately designed to encourage students to pace their reading throughout the school year. From the first
day of school students learn that they will be invited to this party *if* they Title Trek
the number of books equivalent to their grade level. These are the books read
during the school year, over and above classroom assignments. Sandwich this

information into the library orientation speech in September. A few reminders are necessary. Classroom teachers use this incentive to get their classes reading.

Such year-end inducements stir up lots of interest. In the preceding fall a 7th-grade student may assert, "This year I'm going to the party. I'm reading seven books. I've already done two, only five more to go," they'll blabber. At these moments my not-so-sweet side comes out. "So do it. Let me see those entries," I'll counter. Depending on the student, I may roll my eyes in feigned exasperation and mutter, "Yeah, yeah. I'll believe it when I see it." The *tough cookie* attitude keeps students interested. Far better to keep them off guard than for you to plead.

It's a difficult call, but balancing your attitude between the cajoling and the bristly is important. You won't always get it right. The older teens may need a bit more sensitivity as they straddle the precarious beam of self-consciousness, having never turned in a Title Trek and fearing it's the same thing as a book report. Or they may be balking over the principle of trying something so overtly "academic". Then there are the overly bubbly students who just want to yammer on and on over the idea, but can't sit down to write a word. They are all children who can and will do this program if the perfect ploy is used. The angles are as plentiful as the personalities. Children want to succeed, and Title Trekking is an independent, nonjudgmental, nongraded, personal endeavor—yet it is work and it has an intellectual association. Should they take the risk, it's a challenge that students are proud of accomplishing. It offers a structured design that will push them to achieve and the community to applaud.

There will be older students who don't want anything to do with it. That happens. It may sting, but don't take it personally. Many of these same students will read books from the Title Trek lists while openly refusing to journal them. Reckon with this simple fact: These students may not be outwardly participating in the program, but they are reading books that they would otherwise be missing if such a program did not exist in your school. The very existence of a reading incentive program has multiple benefits that you won't always be able to quantify. Having children enjoying reading is the only proof I need.

THE POINT IS?

If you haven't skipped this chapter because you're too overworked and over-whelmed (not to mention underpaid) with ruthlessly weeding outdated titles, preparing your collection for automation, bar-coding, developing your cooperative collection, submitting your budget, considering new database subscriptions, instructing research classes... well, you know the deal, I'll assume that you're still with me.

For you, the payoff is the investment in learning about and considering the perfect books for your audience, designing and coordinating a structured program that coaxes reading into a schoolwide pastime, and having written conversations about carefully selected titles with your students and staff. How bad is that? On the surface it seems like work, but what's the definition of work? Lecturing students on not depending on Google and other search engines for all their research needs? Instructing a research class about the value of navigating through a subscription database search? Typing up overdues? Reshelving books?

Or being overrun with students begging for another good book? Encouraging a child to become a lifelong reader is what I love doing.

Chapter 8

READER'S WORKSHOP: STORY TIME ENHANCEMENT FOR YOUNG ADULTS

Getting students to read can feel like getting a dog to bathe. No matter how much the dog stinks, she doesn't care and wags her tail in dumb indifference. Yet, you've noticed and it's a problem. Between 1982 and 2002 literary reading among adults had fallen 17 percent in the 18–24 age group.[1] All the analyzing and justifying isn't going to change the stats. It's time to take action, be aggressive. In keeping with the analogy, it's time to give the dog a bath. The dog doesn't know she's offensive, any more than students realize (or care) that they're missing out on reading. You need to get their attention if you want their participation.

Trade the bath for a river and fling sticks for the dog to plunge in after in self-propelled glee. You will have changed the dread into self-motivated pleasure. Sneak a capful of shampoo into the mix and the aftermath is all the sweeter. For your students, dispel the preconception that reading is boring and replace it with reading is fun. Fling out a collection of wild ideas, notions, humor, horror, fantasy, romance, and drama and watch students discover what shakes them up. Like that dreaded doggie bath, students suspicious of reading need an appealing introduction to books before their attitude of distaste transforms into enjoyment. And, if you sneak in some literature appreciation, the aftermath is all the sweeter.

Children love "story time" in elementary school. Taking that piece out of their upper school education places an inordinate amount of pressure on students who struggle with independent reading skills. For students who enjoyed the carefree entertainment of a collective read-aloud, exchanging it for independent silent reading is like whipping the blanket out from under them. For such students, reading becomes a source of drudgery, struggle, and often failure. For them, it's no wonder that literature is deliberately avoided and abandoned once it becomes an independent venture loaded with struggle, humiliation, and intellectual risk. Regarding reading aloud to young children, *Horn Book* editor Roger Sutton writes, "The real question is this: even if reading aloud to your kids had no impact on their test scores, would you stop doing it?"[2] If reading aloud to children and young adults helps to initiate, develop, and solidify a love of reading and literature, should we stop doing it?

Jennifer Armstrong, author of *Shipwreck at the Bottom of the World*, has written:

Standards in education seem to be entirely monopolized by the fallacy of false quantification; i.e., if you can't count it, it doesn't count. We can count the number of vocabulary words our children know, the number of metaphors they can pick out, the number of themes identified, and the number of context questions they can answer, but we cannot quantify their response to beauty. So it doesn't count and we don't discuss it. Small wonder, then, that so many children and adolescents do not read for pleasure, joy, or love. They've not been told that pleasure, joy, or love come into it at all, let alone that they come into it from the start.[3]

If we don't take the time to teach students the wonders of literature, why should they take the time to discover it themselves? Committing a weekly 40-minute period to help children experience the pleasure, joy, and love that reading inspires is what Reader's Workshop is all about.

INSPIRING READING

Dedicating a class to instill the pleasures of the written word in our students' lives can bridge the gap between story time and independent reading. When I ask students what Reader's Workshop means to them, they unanimously say, "a time to relax and listen to a story." I love hearing that. I especially love hearing it from teenagers. It's a good description. Reader's Workshop is a relaxing time to enjoy stories.

I then asked them what it was that made Reader's Workshop important—beyond the relaxation part. One student answered, "It helps me with my listening skills. I have a hard time with that, but when you read and I get interested in the story, I can really focus and pay attention." Another said, "I'm a big reader, so I like having a class that's all about books. But Reader's Workshop introduces me to stories that I wouldn't necessarily pick up on my own. Also, you always ask us a lot of questions, and so it makes me think about the book differently than when I just read on my own." I asked them about books-on-tape, curious that if they enjoyed listening to stories, why couldn't they just listen to a tape. You would have thought I lit a fire under them. They got upset, "It's not the same at all. Those voices just drone on. I can't listen to them." Another student added, "That's like having a computer talk at you! You're real and ask us questions." It was also important to them that the class was held in the library, rather than "sitting up straight in uncomfortable chairs at our desks in the classroom."

In essence, Reader's Workshop is a children's and young adult (YA) book club. It is a literature appreciation class that intentionally delivers story to students. It's a read-aloud class using books that are likely to entrance and entertain a listener. For the nonreader, it puts good stories in their lives. For the reader, it puts more good stories into their lives. The other day a teacher brought a most reluctant student in to find a book. He has been in my Reader's Workshop class for several years. He was dragging his feet, but when he saw me he said, "She knows what I like. Let her pick it out." Reader's Workshop helps change the librarian's simplistically perceived role from the person who orders and organizes books in isolation, to the trusted person who knows the best books to read.

It's a class for students to experience the phenomenon of how words communicate and how they have the quiet influence to prompt loud ideas. Most essentially, it's an opportunity for students to discover how connected we all are through the art of written expression. Sometimes it feels that drawing a student's interest toward a roomful of silent titles requires superhero power. Reader's Workshop helps the cause. It proves to students that reading good books is worth it.

SETTING UP A READER'S WORKSHOP

Our Reader's Workshop format is a guided read-aloud class held in the library with individual 4th-, 5th-, 6th-, and 7th-grade classes. Students meet with their English class four times a week and come to the library for Reader's Workshop once a week. These grades have a year-long Reader's Workshop class instruction with the librarian. We coordinate with the curriculum but teach independently. We meet with our 8th- and 9th-grade students in six-week mini-units. Using this staggered single-semester scheduling, we are able to meet with every student in the school. Our 9th-grade classes are taught in a team-teaching format, using the Reader's Workshop time to prepare for author visits and to work in literary circles with the librarian and the English teachers facilitating.

In order to fit this class into the curriculum, we collaborate with other faculty members. At our school, every faculty member submits a semester curriculum map to our dean of faculty. This map provides an outline of the course content, skills taught, key lessons/activities, and the main text and/or literature used. This is made available to all faculty members. It represents an overview of what's being taught throughout the school. Curriculum mapping is an invaluable co-operative tool. It avoids overlapping course content while allowing to collaboratively shore-up skills instruction. These maps help me to select literature to coordinate with classroom themes.

4TH-GRADE MONSTERS AND OTHER FANTASIES

Most schools have a traditional "library time" slot that is typically too rushed and chaotic. Students are ushered into the library to mill about the stacks, tempting one another to distraction, their voices bleating, "Do you have the latest *Series of Unfortunate Events*?" This weekly practice of students hardly listening to a micro-mini-story in ten minutes and then rushing to check out a book before being corralled back to class is, well, unfortunate. The concept is good, but it's time-deprived and thus devoid of substance.

Reader's Workshop takes this same energetic class and collects them into a cohesive group, within a reasonable and relaxed amount of time. They are introduced to books that are certain to entertain and have them begging to hear more. They look forward to the time not merely because they've developed a love for listening to stories, but because they enjoy being listened to as they consider, ponder, and discover the creative process of constructing a story. Push students beyond their passive inclination to be entertained and tap into their creative reserve. Reader's Workshop perpetuates the participatory involvement that enlivens literature. Have students participate by asking questions, and let them create and tell their own stories.

Expecting a roomful of energetic 4th-graders to automatically sit still for a story is a fantasy. With practice and guidance, it does happen. Initially you'll read aloud for 15–20 minutes and allow a brief 5 minutes for students to write, or draw, in response to the reading. Young children sometimes freeze at the writing part, due to feelings of confusion, or simply having a difficult time with the process. Keep the written element simple, brief, and lighthearted. Reader's Workshop is all about loving reading, not about creating obstacles. If a child doesn't want to, or can't, do the written reflection, leave it alone. Gush over the drawing the child has done instead. Hang it up behind your desk. Later in the year, or the following year, this same child will try writing; it just may take him or her a bit longer to grapple with the concept and gain the confidence. Always leave 10 minutes at the end of class for checking out books.

To keep your youngest listeners attentive, use clever strategies. Students love to listen while they doodle. Have boxes of cool colored pencils, crayons, markers, and paper for busy hands. Suggest that they illustrate a cover of their favorite book, or write the title using their own distinctive style. Show them some calligraphy examples from alphabet books. Maybe they'll write their name with a flourish or draw pictures to celebrate an upcoming holiday or author visit. Have pieces of 8½" × 11" paper cut up into fours, and let their creative drawings decorate your next bulletin board. When their hands are constructively busy, students are less fidgety.

READER'S WORKSHOP ACTIVITY FOR 4TH, 5TH, AND 6TH GRADE

Chris Van Allsburgh's *The Mystery of Harris Burdick* (Boston: Houghton Mifflin, 1984) is an excellent example of open-ended storytelling that captivates listeners. It also offers enough intrigue that group discussion and participation is a cinch. And too, it will inspire reluctant writers.

This is the creative tale of illustrator Harris Burdick, who brings his manuscript to a publisher and then mysteriously vanishes. All that is left are his larger-than-life bold paintings and a hint of cryptic captions. Students love to hear the introduction to this book and then take in the pictures to try to puzzle out an ending.

After reading and discussing the unique design of Van Allsburgh's illustrations, have students write their own short story to accompany one of the illustrations. Select one picture for the entire class to work on. As a relatively early-in-the-year choice, there is one of a carving pumpkin scene that fits Halloween. Give students time to craft a story in their journals and then have them share reading them aloud with the class. I always give a child the option of keeping their journal entries private—very few want to.

In a follow-up class, let students select their own favorite illustration about which to write separate stories. I've used this exercise for many years with many different age groups. It's a foolproof favorite. The only problem with this one is that it's difficult to get them to *stop* writing.

UPPER GRADES: TOO DEEP? TOO COOL? WHO KNEW?

In middle and high school the academic demands on class time increase. Reader's Workshop becomes more difficult to fit in. Yet, 7th-grade students just entering the social combat zone have overwhelmingly convinced me of the value of keeping Reader's Workshop in middle school. They arrive to class on time, eager, and attentive. They leave reluctantly, lingering over new books out on the table, getting excited about new titles, and showing an interest that we've craved to establish. When it's time to change classes, they collectively whine, "No! Keep reading. We can be late." They love being read aloud to and are excited to continue discussing the reading. They will keep it going, and going, if you don't take a stand. I'm a kindred spirit, and it is difficult to stop once you have teens hanging on your every word. But I'm not an idiot. I know that listening to a story beats math class. Yet I also see their enthusiasm and the genuine underlying excitement of wanting to hear more of the story. I suffer my share of faculty disapproval when my classes run late.

Sven Birkerts writes, "I am talking here not about reading for information, for facts, but rather the kind of literary reading that NEA's [National Endowment for the Arts] survey measured: the reading of artistic works—novels, poetry, plays and reflective prose that has been written with a care for the language. Immersion in this kind of writing fosters, above all else, linguistic awareness and imagination, and we should linger a moment on each."[4]

Such immersion develops a genuine connection between the librarian and the students. Introduced to authors for the first time in class, students will sidle up to the desk and off-handedly ask for a book recommendation. A trust begins, and the next time they're more confident and direct, "What should I read?" or, "Do you have another one just like this?"

Boys rush the library between classes, grabbing the next sci-fi or fantasy title while repeatedly and plaintively asking, "Is the *Eldest*[5] out yet?" The point is that, if not for a scheduled niche in their academic week, students will miss out on the titles written for them. They'll skip over YA titles to read adult novels from their parents' shelves or the supermarket pocketbooks—if they are reading at all.

READER'S WORKSHOP ACTIVITIES FOR OLDER STUDENTS

In the upper grades the emphasis shifts from predominantly using picture books, humorous novels, or chapter books with dragons and magical themes, to readings from realistic contemporary fiction that uses a variety of writing styles.

- Students are still given paper (I cut 8½" × 11" paper into quarters), and they graduate to the "coolest" markers and art implements to doodle and illustrate with. I collect their work at the end of every class. When I have enough illustrations (and when I have the energy to pull it together) I use their work on the bulletin board outside the library. Often I'll entrust the bulletin board compilation to a couple of my older students.

- Picture books are studied in a more sophisticated vein. We revisit Van Allsburgh's *The Mystery of Harris Burdick* in the 7th grade. Students enjoy this familiar exercise, and their creative writing becomes more elaborate. They may opt to use the story that's in their journal from a previous year, rewriting it, or they may select another illustration to write about.

- The artistic styles, distinctions, and strengths of picture books are discussed. There's conversation about how an independent partnership between an illustrator and author achieves unison. We've used wordless picture books with great success. As with *The Mystery of Harris Burdick*, students write their own interpretation of the wordless books *Time Flies* by Eric Rochman (New York: Crown, 1994) and *Window* by Jeannie Baker (New York: Greenwillow, 1991). ESL students are particularly successful with this exercise. They concentrate on recording their thoughts and feelings, unencumbered by self-imposed inhibitions about what's "good" or "bad" about their writing, unlike their American classmates.

READER'S WORKSHOP LESSON FOR 7TH AND 8TH GRADE

Novel: Jerry Spinelli's *Stargirl* (New York: Random House, 2000)

Timeframe: 40-minute class period, once a week, for one semester. We concentrate on one novel during the semester, interspersed with short stories and preparation for the upcoming author visit.

This lyrical novel works well in a read-aloud class because, like Katherine Paterson's *Bridge to Teribethia* (New York: Crowell, 1977), *Stargirl* has a male and female protagonist that have a strong friendship. It's about adolescent peer pressure versus the spirit of individuality. There are multiple conflicts and themes, which make it another good choice of study. One is a boy's struggle to celebrate the differences of his unique girlfriend, or to conform to the popularity of "normalcy" and squelch the refreshing zest of her free spirit.

In the early part of the year we concentrate on short stories and the effectiveness of metaphors and similes used within the brevity of their content. We then transfer this knowledge to identifying the metaphors and similes used within *Stargirl*—and there are many.

We culminate weeks of reading and discussions with students describing the theme of the novel in a metaphorical phrase.

For this Reader's Workshop, an ESL student from Korea wrote, "Somebody dropped black ink into a clear pond, but it didn't change the color of the pond."

A boy from Arizona wrote, "A pebble in a fast flowing river, worn smooth by the changing current, out of place, and being filed to the 'perfect' shape."

Every student in the class agreed that *Stargirl* was a feel-good novel because of its simplicity, emotional charge, and honesty. They didn't want the story to end. One year a class decided to do a social experiment in our school. They dressed extravagantly, secretly did something kind for another student, or behaved in some dramatically eccentric manner in front of their peers. They wanted to see how it felt to be accepted, or if in fact they would be accepted. They wanted to test if "different" behavior would be automatically rejected and ridiculed by the rest of the school. They wanted to know if being a nonconforming free spirit might prove positively infectious. When we grouped together for our Reader's Workshop class we talked about the results and the feelings generated from their peer's reactions.

This summer I met a past student from that class. She is from Guatemala and is now 17 years old. She ran to greet me with a hug, "Oh, Alison, do you have a book for me to read? Remember *Stargirl*?!" she cooed, her hand to her heart. Those are the resonating and long-lasting impressions that Reader's Workshops can inspire.

READER'S WORKSHOP AND COLLABORATIVE PLANNING

A 7th-grade Adirondack geography class was studying survival stories. The teacher had scooped up from the shelves every outdoor adventure book, including all of Gary Paulsen's novels. It was the opportune moment for me to use Gary Paulsen's young adult autobiography, *How Angel Peterson Got His Name*

(New York: Wendy Lamb, 2003), in their Reader's Workshop class. We spent time considering the setting and time period of Paulsen's autobiography and discussed whether similar risk-taking and daredevil behavior might go on today. We had conversations about how Paulsen's real personality effectively contributed to creating the characters in his novels. This led us to a renewed discussion on how authors use "their own voice" and how doing so makes their fiction credible.

The language arts curriculum is bogged down with implementing state standards. There's hardly enough sanctioned time to teach prose, plays, poetry, writing composition, vocabulary skills, and grammatical skills; fit in a few classics, a quick intro to Shakespearean sonnets; not to mention to prep kids for the new essay component on the SATs and help them draft their secondary school or college applications. Faculty members do not have the immediate awareness of the newest titles in the library's collection, nor do they have the librarian's extensive background experience and knowledge. Reader's Workshop is designed to work in concert with the language arts curriculum, underscoring and embellishing the literary element. It ripples literacy into other areas of the curriculum as well, but its foremost goal is to make reading appealing.

As two separate entities with a similar mission, the librarian and the English department collectively and cooperatively plan their literature units together. The English curriculum integrates Reader's Workshop into their literature component to make the most of its intent, without disrupting or short-changing their curriculum. When students come to the library once a week in place of their English class, a tremendous amount of advanced collaborative planning is in place. If English teachers are using short stories, I augment their unit by reading contemporary short stories aloud. I remain a free agent, staying independent so that the Reader's Workshop complements the curriculum and doesn't mirror, or worse, duplicate it. Here's an example:

> The English class was working on poetry and creative writing. In Reader's Workshop, we read Sharon Creech's *Heartbeat* (New York: Harper Collins, 2004). Students wrote free-verse essays in their journal. If you do this, keep it a short and painless exercise, 10–15 minutes of writing time. For some students, the short amount of time will be the most daunting part of the task. I coach them in advance to take an ordinary incident that happened to them within the past 24 hours. It could be a delicious meal, a fun moment with a friend, a climactic moment on the sports field, or a cataclysmic moment on the sports field. They'll be begging to read their own essays aloud to one another. I was surprised in our Workshop when they asked to read their poems aloud at the schoolwide assembly. We agreed that a presentation could be made, if they were willing to devote additional time to work on their essays. Back in their classroom, their English teacher had them use their drafts, revising and polishing them into a final copy. Then we scheduled a class visit and they presented their free-verse essays to the younger Reader's Workshop class that had been reading Sharon Creech's *Love That Dog* (New York: Harper Trophy, 2001).

Let Reader's Workshop empower the English curriculum. Another example is to use a future visiting author's short story in your class to introduce and immerse students in the author's work, while continuing to look at the defining structure of short story writing. I select short stories by authors whose novels they've heard of (or read), either from me, or as an English assignment. We have discussions concentrating on the elements of short story construction including symbolism, irony, foreshadowing/flashback, setting, and/or point of view. (See Integrating Literature into the Curriculum, Chapter 5, for examples on using author autobiographies, novels-in-verse, multicultural literature, poetry, and fiction within the curriculum.)

Some of our class deliberately reiterates the English department's underpinnings, highlighting the "how" of literary expression, but I don't pummel technique and structure to death. Students warn me when I'm leaning too ardently toward instruction at the expense of the story. If your students are wide-eyed and hanging onto the story, don't kill it by overanalyzing.

Stay attentive toward what you've worked hard to develop: students attracted toward the routine of reading together, voicing their ideas and feelings, discussing the nuances of language, the poetic phrases, the symbolism, the pathos, the reality, the fantasy, the parallel story lines, their connection with characters, their separation from the characters . . . well, you get the idea. You've wicked your passion for literature into these kids. Learning to understand how stories communicate is different from dissecting them. When it feels like too much time is being spent on analyzing or when you sense the class is becoming frustrated and you may be breaking the flow of the story, pull in your reins. "Just read!" they'll beg. Don't worry that you may not be providing enough "instruction." The fundamental purpose of Reader's Workshop is to develop, awaken, or revive children's love for literature. Kindle the passion; don't douse it.

LITERATURE IMMERSION

Before noted YA author Janet McDonald's[6] visit, I read *Spellbound* (New York: Frances Foster, 2001) aloud in the 7th-grade Reader's Workshop classes. *Spellbound* is set in Brooklyn, NY, and deals with unwed teen mothers up against downtrodden inner-city life. This is a culturally foreign experience to students who've been raised in a predominantly white suburban and/or rural environment. Students in 6th, 8th, and 9th grade read *Spellbound* in their English or life skills classes. For the English classes that are unable to fit *Spellbound* into their curriculum, I introduce it in our Reader's Workshop class. Janet's other YA novels, *Chill Wind* (New York: Frances Foster, Farrar, Straus and Giroux, 2002), *Twists & Turns* (New York: Frances Foster, 2003), and *Brother Hood* (New York: Farrar, Straus and Giroux, 2004), are used in literary circles in the 9th-grade English class. As team teachers, the librarian and the faculty become collaborative advocates, supporting one another's programs, and taking advantage of special events to maximize their instructional value.

In our Reader's Workshop we worked on identifying the author's voice. We discussed inner-city vernacular and dialect. Reader's Workshop encouraged discussion and processing of the students' impressions. It was the students' active participation that made the class meaningful. They discussed it from their own personal perspective and experiences. A particularly sheltered girl from Dubai, Saudi Arabia, reacted in shock to the character of Raven, the unwed female mother in *Spellbound*. "Oh! This is a bad book. She shouldn't have done that! It's wrong," she said. Another student, from a rural background and raised by a single mom snapped, "Raven's not bad. She just made a bad choice."

When I read *Walk Two Moons* (New York: Scholastic, 1994) aloud, the same girl from Dubai arrived at class whining, "Will it be sad? I hate sad books!" While her classmates shushed her, I tried to calm her apprehension. I even offered to change novels. Soon she was arriving to class early. During the reading she dramatically clutched her arms about herself, sitting on the edge of her seat, wailing, "Hurry up. No, don't stop! We can be late!" She "hated sad" like kids sitting around the campfire hate ghost stories.

The following year, this same sheltered student entered the library looking for J.D. Salinger's *Catcher in the Rye* (Boston: Little, Brown, 1951). She told me, "My grandmother said that this book is STILL being banned in schools. Is that true? Is it good?" Obviously she was ready to reconsider her preconception of "good and bad" characters. The 7th-grader who had reacted like a powder-puff, tiptoeing around any bit of challenging subject matter, had transformed into an 8th-grader with a powerful passion for literature. Throughout the summer and into her second month of the school year, she had already read fifteen books from our reading incentive program's list. Reader's Workshop had cracked the shelter of her protective shell. Once she began, her interest toward reading, and learning, became ravenous.

With all of our grade levels I read aloud Janet's "Zebra Girl" (*Skin Deep*), a short story that confronts racism within the family household. It had a profound effect on students who considered racism a black-and-white or us-versus-them issue. In the Reader's Workshop students heard biographical sketches about Janet that had been written by and/or about her, including bits and pieces from a slick *Oprah* magazine interview. We concentrated on how poverty rankled the lives of the project community and defined its culture. In short, we immersed ourselves in Janet's work and learned how her voice developed.

INTRODUCING YA BOOKS TO YOUNG ADULT KIDS

When asked about whether students were reading his YA autobiography *Hole in My Life* (New York: Farrar, Straus and Giroux, 2002), Jack Gantos replied, "Teachers are under a lot of pressure to stick to the curriculum, and it is difficult for them to introduce a book into their class lessons. They don't want to introduce a book into their curriculum until they vet it first. I think *Hole in My Life* is just traveling the same route as other books that make it onto the core-reading list."[7] Jack might have added that it's a long, circuitous route and it's hit-or-miss whether just such a book might ever land on that list. In the meantime, the students who would enjoy, benefit, or identify most with these experiences may be stumbling through their own pocks-of-life about to fall into bottomless pits.

Reader's Workshop, through the librarian's experience, knowledge, and extensive exposure to contemporary literature, assures that teen-relevant titles like *Hole in My Life* are at least introduced and presented to students. Even if it isn't used as the primary read-aloud selection, a Reader's Workshop class is a place to booktalk such a title. Reader's Workshop gives the librarian the chance to share material with students that otherwise would go unnoticed. YA titles delve into shared realities of conflict, angst, crisis, isolation, tumult, and drama. Peering through such a looking-glass, students can "experience" the adventure, questionable or otherwise, and safely return home for dinner. Reader's Workshop provides an opportunity to launch these books, saving them from terminal shelf life and, more important, helping a youth through a tremulous time of life. Such exposure may avert tragedy by providing a vicarious experience from a safe distance.

The payoff of devoting time to linking students to literature comes from your students. Years after having my class, a Spanish-speaking student from Argentina paid me the supreme compliment, "You know, when I read to myself in English, I still hear your voice." A college student wrote, "I remember the many books you gave me to read. Many of them I was reading during my other classes, but they were wonderful." When college students come for a visit, they start up literary debates that they had left behind years before in a Reader's Workshop class. After my initial pleasure at their fire, I say, "Okay, let it go!"

FIGHTING A NATION'S READING DISORDER

Today more than ever before, there's a constant battery of competitive demand for people's attention. If it's not a tech-glut of information to be sorted through, it's a wave of electronic communication to juggle. College students paying for their expensive educations surreptitiously text-message one another while they're supposedly listening to their professors lecture. We're so over-connected that we can barely pay attention, and the compulsion to stay tuned in is tuning us out.

In an attempt to derail the electronic information train, Reader's Workshop is a concerted effort to call time-out and present the hard copy of the library's attractions. I'm reminded of the student who said, "Reader's Workshop helps with my listening skills by helping me to concentrate and follow the story." Well, duh! When did we, as educators, become so dumb that we took away stories and introduced meds? Was it the speed of life, or was it complacency?

Reader's Workshop welcomes all students into the fold; test scores and academic ranking do not influence the class make-up. ESL students, learning lab, students in remedial classes—all are in one class. The only criterion is age group. Material that is perfect for 4th grade won't necessarily interest older students, and young adult material isn't always appropriate for the younger ones. The class content evolves as the children's collective intellectual development grows. With the read-aloud "workload" on the librarian, students are on a level playing field, being able to listen and enjoy a story without pressure. They're free to absorb and appreciate literature in a comfortable group and risk-free environment. No wonder the frequent reaction to how they feel about Reader's Workshop is: "It's relaxing."

Students try to flatter me by saying Reader's Workshop is their favorite class. I tell them, "It should be! I stand up here reading to you. I do all the work and you get to listen to great stuff! You have the fun part." I side-step the part about their written entries in their reader's response journal (see Reader's Workshop and Journaling, Chapter 9), the creative writing exercises we do, or the in-depth group discussions we have about literature. Their idea of my doing the work is the diamond that changes their hang-up of reading as an onerous activity into a fun and natural one. Teenagers like to be read to. It's not a huge leap of faith to realize that if they love to be read to, they'll take a chance and try to experience the pleasure on their own.

REALITY AND HUMOR

When YA author Janet McDonald spoke with students, they were very curious about her project "homeland." One bright African-American student asked, "Did you feel you couldn't become a lawyer or writer, or did you think that you'd always live in the projects and have a project booty?" Janet jumped up, displaying her svelte self, and challenged, "You think I have project booty?!" It was a momentous and ice-breaking moment.

During a break in her presentations, Janet visited our Reader's Workshop class. She asked a student what it was all about. Without a pause he said, "Nothing. She just reads to us." I was speechless—but I didn't strangle him.

Janet seized the moment and ran with it. She found a dicey bit of dialogue rich with project dialect and put the selection into my hands.

There I was, Madam White Librarian, blushing while snapping out Aisha and Raven's ghetto-girl lines and tripping over my humility in front of my class, the interviewing newspaper reporter, and the original Project Girl, Janet. Kids loved it. They teased me for months, even a year later. Such moments make your classes memorable and fun.

The other day the same student who said, "Nothing. She just reads to us," stopped me in the hall. He's now in 8th grade. He asked, "When will we get to have Reader's Workshop again? It was my favorite class." Again, I still didn't strangle him.

READING ALOUD THE RIGHT STUFF

Sure-thing titles for your class should include some basic components: First, they must read aloud well and have lots of dialogue. Adventurous, action-packed, and entertaining are important attributes, and humor is always a good choice. Short stories that can be read in a single class period are a good way to begin. Jack Gantos's "Jack Henry" titles are a knock-out hit for middle-schoolers. Each chapter reads like a short story cycle. *Always* read the material before reading it aloud to your class. For instance, Gantos will rattle an ill-prepared adult reader with his graphic antics. One of my coworkers who hadn't read her chapter in advance was alarmed by the tale of the cat chopped-up in the engine, among others. She accused, "This guy's a maniac! The kids loved it." There are great resources from which to suggest titles, or from which to pull selections, including Jim Trelease's well-used *The Read Aloud Handbook* (New York: Puffin, 2001) and Jon Scieska's *Guys Write for Guys* (New York: Viking, 2005). If you're new to reading aloud, don't hesitate to rely on pre-tested suggestions.

Practice reading aloud. If this is your first experience with having a read-aloud class, don't take on all grades. Begin with the younger classes and work your way up. Some of the classic children's novels that you're apt to be more familiar with are excellent read-aloud selections. You'll get a kick out of reading Roald Dahl's *The B.F.G.* (New York: Farrar, Straus and Giroux, 1982) and Sid Fleischman's *The Whipping Boy* (New York: Greenwillow, 1986). They are lots of fun. Concentrate on reading slowly. It will sound slow to your ear, but for the listener it takes a moment to get into their hearing range, circulate around, and settle in. Give your students enough time to wrap their cognitive skills around the words, letting the sentences transform into images that percolate into and spark their imagination.

There's a tendency to overdramatize, or become overly theatrical when reading aloud, particularly with dialogue. Be cautious about doing this. If you put too much of yourself into energizing the story, you risk tampering with the author's original intent. Leave the drama to the author who created it and for the listener to interpret. This is not to say you shouldn't be expressive and articulate. The more reading aloud you do, to various age groups, the more comfortable you'll become with straddling the fine line between expressive and inventive. You'll reach that mystical moment when you become the medium through whom the author's words are channeled. You'll end a chapter, rejoin your quietly attentive audience, and step out of the ethereal zone of story. It's a priceless sensation.

Stay sensitive toward your class's reaction. I recall the time I read L.S. Mathew's *Fish* (New York: Delacorte, 2004) to a class and one of my students kept her head down on the desk, looking sad with despair. This little novel, ambivalent with unspecified gender, setting, time, or place, was rift with the trauma of war on land and people. My student's brother had recently been deployed to Iraq. It was a stupid oversight on my part, however unintentional. You'll make mistakes because it's impossible to know everybody's sensitivities. But students will tell you in subtle ways if the choice is wrong. Most evident will be antsy disruptions: Either the read-aloud choice isn't working or somebody is uncomfortable with the storyline or subject matter. Always have a back-up short story or novel to get through these awkward times.

READER'S WORKSHOP AND THE LIBRARY CONNECTION

Prior to holding Reader's Workshop classes, my students were just a collective part of the school population. They considered me just another puzzled piece of the faculty. Now we communicate on an individual level that is meaningful. There's a mutual connection made by sharing literature.

As you develop your Reader's Workshop class and it becomes increasingly successful, you'll be faced with this problem: How do you get your daily work accomplished? There will be fewer hours to devote to the daily library tasks of inter-library loans, overdues, shelving, weeding, ordering, automating, team meetings, and research instruction, to name some. A constant balancing act will often go akilter. The only insight I may offer is that a Reader's Workshop class will generate energy and stimulate interest in the collection and the library. Without Reader's Workshop that level of interest won't happen, and then why, and for whom, are you doing the daily maintenance? Your unshakable inner resolve of the importance of literature in your students' lives should win over your faculty and administration. Your administration is a good source of support for the daily chores problem. Extra funding for clerical help, a library assistant, an intern, or a volunteer, will help.

Finally, some instruction is better than no instruction. You won't develop an entire program within a year, and you may only do part of a program part of the year. You may start working with one grade and see how it evolves before taking on multiple grades. The positive outcome will be that implementing some literature programming will be a beginning. Your belief, conviction, and effort will help to breathe life into a nation of dormant young readers.

NOTES

1. "Reading At Risk: A Survey of Literary Reading in America," NEA Report 2002.

2. Roger Sutton, editorial, *Horn Book*, Vol. 81, Iss. 4, July/Aug. 2005, p. 391.

3. Jennifer Armstrong, "Greeting Beauty," *Horn Book*, Jan./Feb. 2005, Vol. 81, Iss. 1, p. 57.

4. Sven Birkerts, "The Truth about Reading," *School Library Journal*, Nov. 2004, pp. 50–52.

5. Paoline, Christopher, *Eldest* (New York: Random House, 2005).

6. Janet McDonald, recipient of the Corretta Scott King/John Steptoe Best New Talent Award for *Chill Wind*.

7. Alison Follos, "Gantos Is Seriously Funny," *Library Media Connection*, Jan. 2005, pp. 50–52.

Chapter 9

READER'S WORKSHOP
AND JOURNALING

EXAMINE—EXPRESS—EXPOUND

I believe in journaling. The act of writing forces you to block out extrinsic interruptions and turn inward to express personal observations, opinions, and stories in an uninhibited manner. Writing demands discipline. We are a culture that "protects" our children from discipline because it's difficult and extracts hard work. The perks of our materialistic society—overindulgence, entitlement, and instant gratification—are counterproductive to cognitive development.

Writing requires you to focus, concentrate, capture, and portray an idea. Effective written communication is limited to the complex tool of language. And because single words, standing independent of one another, are one dimensional, it takes commitment to connect them into sentences, phrases, paragraphs, and stories that communicate ideas effectively. Writing requires personal investment, mental engagement, and once again, the most precious of all commodity, *time*. For today's quick-fix temperament, that's a daunting combination: using building blocks of words to create larger-than-life expositions of ideas, visions, and stories. This demands mental engagement and creative insight. In simplistic terms, it requires children to think. The ability to transform squiggles on a page into infinite dimensions of discernable expression is a profound skill.

Most attractive of all is that journal writing is for the student, not for a test score. Krashen states, "First, and most obvious, we write to communicate with others. But perhaps more important, we write for ourselves, to clarify and stimulate our thinking. Most of our writing, even if we are published authors, is for ourselves."[1]

Journaling is a way to slow down the daily pace and make a concerted effort to gather cohesive thoughts and record reflections. Through the writing process an indelible moment is caught. Students that use journal writing to help process thoughts are "forced to show up." As a collective group, they cannot defer to the student who usually serves as the class spokesperson because individually and independently they record their own unique thoughts. With journaling, every student *speaks* their mind.

In Reader's Workshop students are asked to consider underlying themes presented in a reading, interpret them introspectively, and then record their thoughts in their journals. This is a concrete exercise for students to dig in and explore what makes written language effective and fun. The attraction is the entertainment factor and comprehension grows as exposure increases.

At the beginning of the school year, students receive a basic marbled composition book to use as their Reader's Response journal. They'll use this notebook to answer questions at the end of each Reader's Workshop class. It also doubles as their Title Trek journal (see Title Trekking, Chapter 7). Students begin using their journal in 4th grade and continue using them throughout their time at school (4–5 years) or until it is filled. The Reader's Response journal is a chronological record of students' reaction to literature and their original prose and poetry entries that are made during Reader's Workshop classes. It chronicles and summarizes the different books that have been read aloud to them, as well as the books they've logged through their participation in the Title Trek reading incentive program. It is a retrospective portfolio of their literary development and a compilation of annotations about books they've enjoyed.

Recently an 8th-grade student told me, "I was reading my journal the other day. I looked at the first few Title Treks I wrote in 4th grade—and *I* don't even understand what I meant!" I couldn't resist, "Well, think how I feel trying to interpret them?" We both laughed. On the flip side, this student has entered thirty-eight summaries of books that she's read in four years. Her entries are now comprehensive, introspective, and impressive. Additionally, she is a student advocate lobbying to get more free-reading time built into the school day through the student council. When she was a 4th-grader, I recall this student's mother worrying about the fact that her child hated to read.

A large part of the purpose of Reader's Workshop is to discuss literature. The journal format is used for a reader's response to the stories we read together. The Reader's Workshop format promotes looking outward, and ultimately inward, within the safety of literature. The journal is the student's literary diary. Nonetheless, it *is* an academic record, I *will* read it, and my response is directly contingent upon his or her effort.

I repeatedly remind students, "Answer the question to the best of your ability. There is never a right or wrong response when you are reacting to literature: It is your personal opinion. I want you to consider the reading honestly and react personally. The only wrong answer is no effort, or an entry that is completely irrelevant to the reading. In such a case, we'll discuss the problem together. Hearing your classmate's response will help to get your reflective juices flowing." I try to make the writing element do-able and nonthreatening. Journaling is not about creating instructional stumbling blocks. It's about articulating literary preferences. The journaling component intensifies the connection beyond the act of listening and encourages students to exercise their writing and language skills. Journaling prompts students to express their impressions and feelings candidly. I have found that if you let students write what they honestly feel, without judgment, they write.

Students write in their Reader's Workshop journals readily and enthusiastically. Their eager participation demonstrates a desire to articulate their thoughts and expound on their emotional and introspective reactions to literature. After they've captured their responses in their journals, we share them in a group discussion. Interestingly enough, the students most reticent to engage in conversation are often quick to volunteer to read their written entries aloud. Their sensitive reactions to literature dispel their façades of disinterest. They reveal candor and original thinking that they have protectively camouflaged from the teen social scene. From the passion that students pour out, it's apparent that they're hungry to assert their identities, speak their minds, and be listened to.

Their concentration is being battered to smithereens by interruptions from changing classes, hallway gossip, social and familial fluctuations, and all the other disruptions of navigating through their daily lives. Journaling corrals reflections, fortifies concentration, and helps buttress against periphery thoughts.

TIPS FOR SETTING UP THE JOURNALS

- Journals should be simple and informal. Take a basic composition book, place a strip of yellow tape on the bottom of the spine (much like the call number placement), and write a number on it in black Sharpie ink.
- Have a list of the students and jot down their number next to their name for quick reference, because students *will* forget their numbers.
- Shelve the journals in numerical order and in a central location in the library. The number system allows students to quickly find their journals and put them away in an *orderly* manner (if you're lucky).
- Students may take their journals out of the library in order to complete a question, or enter a summary for their Title Trek. Caution students not to let the journals travel too far, or for too long. Journals are lost infrequently, but if students have logged many entries it can be a real calamity when it happens.

GIVE STUDENTS CLEAR GUIDELINES

- Bring a pencil to class (translates to you having a jar of pencils available).
- Written responses must be at least one paragraph and MUST be legible.
- Don't use boring, empty adjectives. Tell me *how* the story was great—not just *that* the story was great, or if the story was funny, what made it so?
- Spelling doesn't matter! (Keep your students excited about writing their interpretations—don't make them self-conscious about spelling. Bonus: It quiets the clamor of, "How do I spell...?")
- Don't give me "yes" or "no" answers. If I ask whether you like the main character, describe why you do or don't.

GIVE STUDENTS GUIDED QUESTIONS

- Do you empathize with the character? If so, why? If not, why not?
- Have you ever had a similar experience?
- Have you ever felt the way this character is feeling?
- Do you think that this story is predictable?
- How do you think it will resolve itself?
- Compare this author's stories to another similar or different book. Do you notice anything unusual or distinctive about his or her writing style? Does anything stand out? Explain.

If abstract, introspective questions are becoming too erudite and you sense your students are about to buckle, switch gears and go simple black and white. Spend a read-aloud class with students recording the metaphorical language, or similes, that they pick out during the reading. Many books lend themselves to this; Jerry Spinelli's *Stargirl* (New York: Random House, 2000), Sharon Creech's *Walk Two Moons* (New York: Scholastic, 1994), and Sid Fleischman's *The Whipping Boy* (New York: Greenwillow, 1986) work well. Though I don't recommend it as a constant practice, this is a concrete exercise that works well when students seem fried and frazzled from the outside forces of their day.

Ask students to share their written responses as a closing exercise. This is always an optional request. If some students are shy, offer to read their response aloud for them. When you run short on time (because students have begged you to read longer than you should have), use their journal entries to open up the next class discussion.

Collect their journals for your review and provide a written response. Students thrive on and deserve a one-on-one written exchange. A response, even of a few words, from you indicates to them that their reflections are valuable and worthy of your time and attention. You'll learn some surprising things. Students you thought were barely paying attention will please you with their astute responses.

When time is a factor, save words and decorate their entry with a sticker. These symbols of approval carry an inordinate amount of value for the sophisticated adolescent. For middle school students whose connection with literature has been weakened and for whom reading has become predominantly a struggle or failure, a Reader's Workshop class can work wonders. Many of these students will experience a renewed affinity for reading in a read-aloud class. Stickers are stars of approval and resuscitate a pride and confidence that's been shrinking and evaporating for these students since they entered school. As children progress through school, not only their skills, but their confidence should too.

THE CONCRETE AND MEASURABLE BENEFITS TO JOURNALING

Journaling:

- Captures free thoughts that a reading stimulates before they dissolve
- Creates a safe place to record free-writes
- Stimulates the disciplined, and routine, practice of writing
- Contributes to strengthened essay skills
- Encourages students to sort through abstract concepts, process them, and express them in their own words
- Allows practice in succinct summarization

Journaling offers the luxurious time to digest literature—to ponder, scrutinize, and absorb it. A connection develops between the reader and an author. The quality of the author's work is amplified and reiterated as students consider a literary work, clearly record their thoughts, and then discuss them within a Reader's Workshop class.

JOURNALING THROUGHOUT THE SCHOOL

Our faculty wanted to use journals throughout the curriculum. We wanted students to embrace the daily habit of recording journal entries and to understand their value. In the overall school curriculum students were taught, encouraged, and assigned to use daily journals. Students' entries ranged from reflections on field trips to reactions to biology lab experiments. The following describes how we collectively implemented journal practices within the English and Reader's Workshop curriculums.

In English class and Reader's Workshop classes, students in 5th–9th grade read (or were read) Jack Gantos's *Joey Pigza Swallowed the Key*. In an era when ADHD is a normal learning dysfunction (a disturbing oxymoron) and Ritalin is relied on like a butterfly bandage, Joey Pigza is an identifiable literary character for children of all ages. Students have either known a "Joey" in their class, or they *are* Joey.

The following questions encouraged students to respond to this book:

- Have you ever been in a similar situation?
- Do you think the character wanted to misbehave?
- What are the family relationships like? Are they close? Are they supportive of one another? If so, explain. If not, where is there conflict?
- What is it that makes the family relationships feel so intense?
- What was the conflict that Joey wrestled with? Are there more than one? If so, what are they?
- Might this same conflict crop up again, or is it tidily packed away for good?
- Can you describe something about the writing style that convincingly portrays Joey?
- Is this story funny? Why?
- Is this story sad? Why?
- Can something be funny and sad? Explain.

Again, when you ask students to journal, throw in an occasional tangible exercise, especially for students who struggle with abstract concepts or fear personalizing the material. Before beginning a reading, ask students to write down any distinctive examples of creative language: strong vocabulary? original style? dialect? similes? metaphors?

JOURNALING IN READER'S WORKSHOP

Jack Gantos's distinctive writing style was introduced to the students at my school by reading aloud a number of what he has described as "autobiographical-fiction story cycles" about his alter-ego, Jack Henry. Students learned that these stories emerged from Jack's childhood journal entries. I read several excerpts from *Jack Adrift: Fourth Grade without a Clue* (New York: Farrar, Straus and Giroux, 2003), *Jack on the Tracks: Four Seasons of Fifth Grade* (New York: Farrar, Straus and Giroux, 1999), and *Heads or Tails: Stories from the Sixth Grade* (New York: Farrar, Straus and Giroux, 1994). Students identified with Jack Henry's preoccupation with finding his balance within his family circle while simultaneously suffering the trials and tribulations of school life. Through correspondence with the author they learned that many of the experiences and the feelings in the stories stemmed from real life. They begged me to read more. We concluded the Jack Henry stories with selections from *Jack's Black Book* (New York: Farrar, Straus and Giroux, 1997) and *Jack's New Power, Stories from the Caribbean Year* (New York: Farrar, Straus and Giroux, 1995). These stories notably shift Jack's character development as he grows up. Students used their journals to consider and interpret a variety of writing techniques and styles used. Here are some examples:

- What have you noticed about the changes in writing style from chapter to chapter?
- What did you notice about the changes in style from book to book?
- What do you think were realistic and true events, and what might have been embellished events?
- What is your interpretation of "real fiction"?
- Compose a paragraph of "real fiction" from something that's happened in the past twenty-four hours. It could have happened to you, or could have occurred around you.
- Gantos shifts from first-person narrative to dialogue. Do you think this is an effective technique? Why or why not?
- Gantos has the trademark of using humor to deflect attention from the underlying seriousness of a situation. Provide examples of when this occurred. How did the author make it appear funny? What were some of the buried emotional feelings that the humor masked?

This demanded pretty heavy literary awareness from middle school students. They peeled back the layers and delved beyond plot description. They discovered character depth and literary agility. They began to understand what creates a good story, and best of all, they loved it.

When Jack Gantos visited our school, we capitalized on his winning and influential presentation to inspire and elevate our students' investment in journaling. Jack told students:

> I write in my journal every day. Don't try to write a novel. First write a little bit every day. Start with 15–20 minutes a day. Writing is a cumulative process and eventually those daily entries will become stories. I love journals because you can be sneaky. I overhear conversations at restaurants, airports; I even find material from graveyards. Joey Pigza's name [*Joey Pigza Swallowed the Key*, New York: Farrar, Straus and Giroux, 1998] came from a tombstone I saw while driving around with my mother.[2]

A few days after his presentation, a 9th-grade boy was sitting outside of the library. He greeted me first thing in the morning, "I'm writing in my journal. I'm going to do this every day. Jack inspired me," he earnestly announced.

Journaling had gone from a required assignment to a self perpetuated interest. For some students, it became a daily discipline. For a greater number of students, it became an academic routine that was completed willingly, creatively, and without reservation. The "blank page" ceased to be an insurmountable challenge as students were encouraged to log more and more free-writes without being repressed by criticism or assigned a grade. While students are the first to groan, "She writes me endless questions!" they are also quick to check back in the library to see what I've written in response to their entry. They willingly investigate the multiple angles of literature. As with reading, I want them to love written communication, not be turned off by it. I know it has worked because instead of forcing students to journal in my classes, I have to insist that they put their pencils *down*!

NOTES

1. Stephen D. Krashen, *The Power of Reading* (Westport, CT: Libraries Unlimited, 2004), p. 137.

2. Alison Follos, "Jack Gantos on Writing: Digging Up Creative Juices from Restaurants to Graveyards," *Children & Libraries*, Summer/Fall 2005, Vol. 3, Iss. 2, pp. 42–44.

Chapter 10

VISITING AUTHOR PROGRAM

In our lives of instant gratification an author visit epitomizes the persuasive and long-lasting effects of literary immersion. Author visits make connections between students, faculty, and the librarian. The very presence of the author underscores the value your school places on literature. The visit produces the positive effects of breathing new life into a stale curriculum, jazzing up a routine semester, and inspiring everyone to read. Who better to provide convincing testament to the passion, power, and profession of literature than an author? The visit may be a single day, but it will create interest in the author's work for several years and, more intrinsically, will positively influence students' opinions about literature.

Our tiny school in rural New York has had the privilege of hosting children's and young adult (YA) authors for many years. We've had a variety of different personalities with varying degrees of success. But there has never been a visit that wasn't worth the effort—though some were more dramatic than others. Jack Gantos had a problem with our *rotten* 50-degrees-below-zero extreme weather. Tim Wynne-Jones, a neighbor from northern Canada, didn't even flinch when the power went off. Only the lack of an extreme sense of humor will dash the spirit of an author visit.

AUTHOR VISITS MAKE A DIFFERENCE

Author visits impact the entire school community. Visiting author Janet McDonald, who exposes the highs and woes of her personal life in her adult memoir *Project Girl*, said, "If everyone told the complete truth, other people would know that they all have a shared experience." Students agreed and reacted to Janet's visit with surprised candor, remarking, "It seems like authors just write books, then disappear, but when you meet a real live author and she's talking about music and sports, you say, 'Wow!' They're like normal people. It's amazing." Another reflected, "I thought she would be more poised, but she was really fun and exciting. She inspired me because she went out for what she believed in—and succeeded." An 8th-grader who sports a haughty and aloof posture wrote, "I pictured her being a tough project girl with a lot of attitude. Well, I was wrong. I learned a lot more about her and her life. Like how she has two sides: one smart side and the other, a mix of funny and enthusiastic. I enjoyed having her here and a lot of kids seemed to relate and like her. Now, since I've met her, I really want to pick up another one of her books."

A prime example of the emotional effects that an author's visit might have on students was witnessed in a packed library of 5th- and 6th-graders. Students had been wrestling with racism, a chronic topic that arose in our multicultural literature unit. Visiting author Janet McDonald[1] confronts issues of racial and cultural prejudices within most of her literature. For four months prior to her visit, over and over again in English classes, world cultures classes, and in our weekly Reader's Workshop class, we discussed race, culture, values, preconceptions, misconceptions, and differences. Students read Janet's short story "Zebra Girl" (*Skin Deep*), which deals with racism within a single family, one sister pitted against the other because of skin tone. Students from 6th–9th grade read *Spellbound*, the first in Janet's trilogy about New York City (NYC) teens breaking free from the welfare habit. They also knew biographical details about Janet's *Project Girl* climb from the ghettos of NYC to the intellectual splendor of practicing international law in Paris, France. They were ready for her visit.

To provide you a case-in-point, example one student began talking about the particularly funny "project booty" referenced in *Spellbound*. She asked, "Did you feel that you would ever become a lawyer, or did you think you would always live in the projects and have a project booty?" Later, after the laughter died, this same student referred to the short story "Zebra Girl." With her dark skin glowing and her eyes bold and steady, she shared how she was always called the "darkest one" in her home. She stated, "When my sister says that I look like charcoal, it makes me want to punch her face in." Such moments highlight the empowerment that authors instill in us. As Janet remarked later, "When you share the hard truths about your background, you hit a chord with other people. You learn that other people have felt the same way, or done similar things."

Storyteller and wilderness survival expert Jim Bruchac grew up surrounded by Native American cultural tales and storytelling. Jim said, "I swore I would *never* tell those 'silly stories.' Never say never and never say always." After Jim's visit to North Country School (NCS) students wrote, "I really like how he inspired me to learn more about the outside. I would like him to teach me more about how he is able to express himself and create the stories." Another student remarked, "Sort of like Janet, I thought he had a way different appearance and attitude than I expected. I thought he would have long black hair with some ancient jewelry made out of beads—with a 'don't mess with me' kind of attitude. But he was nice, he had short hair, and he was tall and cautious."

The above students' quotes demonstrate with clarity and certainty how dramatically an author is able to elevate perceptions of, and interest toward, his or her work.

FINDING THE RIGHT AUTHOR FOR YOUR SCHOOL

Selecting the right author is important. Your decision will be driven by your budget. If you have substantial funding for a Visiting Author Program, you may be able to invite two authors: a children's author for the younger grades, and a young adult author for the older students. Otherwise, you need to assess your school's population and establish who will be able to speak to the whole school. Not every author will be a perfect fit with every age group. Though their literature may not be appropriate for all ages, ideally, you'll want somebody who is comfortable presenting to all grades. It's a big expense and a major personality that you're bringing into your community. Strive to include everyone. If a young children's author is visiting, think of a way to creatively involve the upper grades. Maybe the author has experience with storytelling? Older students are fascinated by the art of storytelling. They particularly love scary stories. When Jim Bruchac shared his native tales, our 9th-grade students continued to mimic him, chanting, "Hey!" and then responding, "Ho!" during evening hide-and-seek field games months after his visit.

When I book our visiting author I discuss not only our programming but our expectations. If I'm only able to afford one author for the entire school, then there will be several different presentations geared toward several different age groups—usually three to four separate presentations.

YA authors are not necessarily prepared to present to young students. My conservative creed is to never assume. I don't want my YA presenters to feel overly controlled, but I need them to know that I have vulnerable, innocent, and very young 3rd- and 4th-grade students. As a boarding school, we must consider our "parenting" role toward our children. I expect a responsible attentiveness toward all students.

If a YA author is visiting your school, involve the elementary grades through hands-on experiences. Suggest to your YA author to bring copies of their galleys, cover art, manuscript drafts, journals, translations, etc. Carol Plum-Ucci[2] came to our school and she delighted our younger students with edge-of-their seats scary slumber-party type stories. When notably banned and challenged YA author Chris Crutcher[3] visited, he avoided his issue-oriented subject matter with the younger students, concentrating instead on notoriously comical tales from his childhood. Typically it won't be how much to include, but what you may need to exclude, that you'll need to concentrate on.

YA author Janet McDonald planned a poetry workshop for the younger students. They worked on haikus, read them aloud, and enjoyed one another's reactions. They also spent time asking Janet questions about her life. YA authors will also discuss the mechanics of getting a book published, story construction, cover art, collaboration with an illustrator, layouts, submissions, and, what students find the most interesting of all, rejections. Most authors are happy to include all grades, and as Jack Gantos once commented, "It's just common sense that when speaking to primary grades I focus on primary level topics, and on up the ranks."[4]

Attend conferences where you can observe authors in panel discussions or storytelling presentations. Make sure that you collect their business cards. This alleviates the time-consuming footwork on your part when you are back at school and ready to contact authors about a visit. Don't count on being able to contact them through publishers, agents, their web pages, or published e-mail addresses. It can be a deflating endeavor to the most tenacious spirits. A one-on-one conversation with your prospective guest at a workshop or conference is your best chance of securing a sound contact. My theory is that e-mail has made everyone more contactable and accessible, rendering authors overrun with correspondence, and thus, ironically, less communicative.

Expect to pay anywhere from $500 to $3,500 toward the author's honorarium. How much do authors charge? How much do you have? You'll need to factor in lodging costs, meals, and travel expenses. If funds are tight, consider regional authors. Their schedules are more flexible because they don't have to allow for several days of travel, and their fees are often more reasonable as a result. Also, you'll be able to significantly reduce the travel and lodging expenses. You might also consider "sharing an author" with another school, although this is a strain on the author and it demands more organizational time on your part. I don't like to share authors, but if it makes the difference between an author visiting or not, I will. In fact, after hosting authors for sixteen years, this year I shared Chris Crutcher and James Bruchac with the local public school. It allowed us to invite two authors.

Some authors will work with you on the rates; others are clearly nonnegotiable. Get this settled from the start. You don't want muddy financial issues to strain the event. Usually, you're able to have the author submit their travel expenses in advance (flight, rental car, etc.). There have been times when we've reimbursed for travel expenses after the presentation. The bottom line is, don't place a guest in the awkward predicament of having to ask for their money: Have the author's check ready.

Speak with colleagues about their experiences with past author visits. Find out from your colleagues who worked well for them. Not every great writer is cut out for public speaking. The reality is that many of them aren't. I've been able to select our guests through first-hand attendance at speaking engagements, but one colleague of mine wasn't so lucky, and commented, "Many of ours have been duds." This would be a dreadful situation for all, and certainly not favorable for the reading interest that you're trying to promote. It's valuable to network with colleagues and find out who has connected well with their students. If you're unable to attend conferences where you can personally observe presentations, you'll definitely want to solicit recommendations from other librarians who do attend.

THE HIGHLIGHTS

After several years of successful visits hosted on a shoestring budget, I lobbied our school administrators to establish a concrete visiting author budget. Having many successful events convinced them of the program's merit within the curriculum. Canceling the visits would have been a huge loss. A small budget was established for the program, but it was a huge beginning. Our Visiting Author Program (VAP) was secure. Having a budget in place alleviates the inordinate amount of stress of trying to arrange a visit when capital is contingent on fund raising. Aggressive fund raising demands obviously sap lots of attention away from the daily library program.

BENEFITS FROM THE VISIT

1. *The inspiration factor for students*. Students are bursting with creative and fresh ideas. Authors have a knack for extracting that creativity and encouraging kids to use it. Often it's the author's own hapless tales from his or her life, explaining why they became a writer, that will spark the wick.
2. A writer's visit transforms written passages privately interpreted by an independent reader into a shared and expounded group discussion.
3. A visiting author shows that writing is a vocation and not a mystical gift.
4. Students grasp the value of learning basic writing skills in order to produce an artful and expressive end product.

5. The visits reveal the exciting, and surprising, personality of the person hidden between the covers.

6. Authors who personally deliver their stories break language barriers. Tim Wynne-Jones[5] visited our school and he gave a little girl from Japan his short story collection *The Book of Changes* (New York: Orchard, 1995) in her native Japanese language. With this gift, her face glowed, and in return she gave him a hug of thanks. She attended his first presentation with faltering comprehension. Nonetheless, she also attended his second session. Tim's presence, and present, bridged the foreignness of language.

7. Writers who visit students and describe the ropes of the profession—their dreams, failures, daily routine, structure, writing habits, grueling number of drafts, submissions, rejections, and at-long-last, publications—demonstrate, in tangible terms, the reality of the market. YA author Jack Gantos shared with students that writing is hard work, "not just wicked work, but a lot of it is Eureka work."

8. Authors teach students by example that real-life experiences are the well of material for stories. Many authors have autobiographies and/or memoirs that they are happy to discuss with students. More than any English assignment does, these conversations inspire students to keep reading and start writing.

9. Students respect and honor an exchange with a published author. They appreciate and thrive from the opportunity.

10. *Inspiration factor for faculty*. We all benefit from new interactions with colleagues, which is why we're encouraged to attend professional development workshops (which entail big travel and registration fees). A special staff workshop should be planned to provide professional growth and development for the entire faculty. When Chris Crutcher visited, we held a special evening professional development workshop. We invited librarians, administrators, and interested educators throughout our region. We began with a reception that allowed colleagues to visit and network. Then Chris presented a question-and-answer session about the social, cultural, gender, and racial issues that he tackles in his literature. The workshop pivoted around the rationale for exposing teens to heated issues in YA literature.

Because our school is small and isolated, the advantages of being able to invite the public to special events has powerful consequences. It gives our faculty exposure to the area public school educators and it showcases the unique, creative, and instructional impact of education outside of the public sector's standards and mandates. After we hosted a professional workshop with Michael Sullivan, a public school colleague confided, "I love your school. You could really tell how everyone is very different from each other, and you may not always get along, but you come together and really care about the students. It made me so bummed-out to have to return to my school." Despite her spoken dissatisfaction, she went away with new teaching practices. She was able to introduce refreshing possibilities into her educational community. She was quick to register when we hosted our next professional development workshop.

HOLDING A WRITER'S WORKSHOP: INSTRUCTIONAL INSPIRATION

An author visit elevates the level of educational instruction for all. Most guests have a generous reserve of degrees and published works. They've often taught creative writing classes at major college and/or universities. Some of our visiting authors have served as resident creative writing instructors at the most prestigious children's literature and writing programs in the country. Being in a classroom is familiar turf for many authors. Take advantage of their expertise.

It often takes somebody fresh to enter your school—acting outside the snarl of in-school politics—to revitalize teaching ideas and stir up creative excitement. Having an author visit refreshes faculty and helps them to refocus and to resuscitate stale and stagnant lesson plans. Many authors are willing to share their successful writing techniques within a planned and well-organized environment.

Faculty attending the presentation gain:

Novel motivating and revitalizing classroom techniques

New creative writing tips to add pizzazz to their classroom teaching

A professional relationship that revives their energy, faith, and interest in education

Inspiration from conversations and interactions with the author

Renewed confidence to take risks and inspire original thinking and writing from their students

If you have the time to run one, a Writer's Workshop is potentially the most rewarding interaction that students will have with the author. Host this workshop during the final session of the author's visit. This eliminates any ice-breaking need as students will have already attended the author's presentation, have had some question-and-answer time, and have had the opportunity to engage in casual conversation. The Writer's Workshop is a specific and extended moment in which to receive professional feedback on their work. The workshop can range from a sensitive exchange within a group setting on their poetry or essays, to a story-prompting session of word play, brainstorming, and discussions on literary tricks, skills, and developing routine practices.

When I asked Jack Gantos if having an author visit his school would have made any difference in his life, he responded:

> It would have helped me to focus on the goals of a writer. It would have been instructive to listen to a person tell how they organize their lives, their reading lists, their writing day and how they set goals that they try to reach. Writers provide insight into the elements of writing and bleed off a lot of the "myth" of writing. This is a step-by-step job: a blue-collar job, and not some muse-driven exercise in fluffy expression. I would have *loved* to be encouraged to take myself seriously as a young man, and, simply, to realize that as a job in life, you *can* become a writer. Not one person during my education ever said that writing fiction was a career I could aspire toward. Instead we had bike mechanics and pilots come and speak at our school.[6]

About the Writer's Workshop, a student wrote, "It was more exciting than I thought it would be, and I had my hopes up pretty high! The Writer's Workshop was fun because usually when you have an author come they tell you about themselves and their book(s) then they leave. But this time Janet got to hear what I had to say, as well as read my writing!! She complimented me on my writing which was very flattering. It was the first time I have ever talked with a published author before. I think that this experience will inspire me to write more." Without exception, each year when I announce the future author that will be visiting, students ask, "Will they hold a Writer's Workshop?" (Oh yes, they also ask me why I don't get J.K. Rowling.)

In order to assure the one-on-one dialogue that contributes to the personalized instruction and long-lasting impressions that a Writer's Workshop generates, attendance must be select and numbers limited. The workshop is geared toward upperclassman and covers age-appropriate content for the discussions that will transpire. Remind underclassman (and their teachers) griping about not being allowed to participate in the Writer's Workshop that their time will come. Younger students will have their opportunity in future years.

Acceptance into the workshop should be narrowed to students who have submitted a completed work and are willing to share it with a group. Collaborative measures with the author and the English department in advance will establish submission criteria. I serve as the intermediary, hammering out the details and putting it all together. This extensive planning guarantees an optimal event.

Encourage staff members to attend. During Tim Wynne-Jones's visit our staff learned creative writing games that continue to be used in the classroom years later. He demonstrated use of anagrams, acrostics, palindromes, pangrams, and more. Two years later a student asked, "Will we be able to have a Writer's Workshop with this year's author? I really liked the creative writing class that Tim Wynne-Jones did with us." When such random feedback trickles down through layers of the educational quagmire, pay attention.

ADVANCED AUTHOR PREPARATION

Some authors are so seasoned that all you'll need to do is show up. That's the exception. It's better to err on the side of being overly prepared. Have a give-and-take approach, advising your guest of the school's curriculum and the student body, and helping them to customize their presentation to suit your faculty's expectations.

Negotiate an author visit months in advance: availability, dates, honorarium, and travel, and then hone in on the fine details. E-mail correspondence is "the bomb," as my students say. Strong collaborative work prior to the visit is well accomplished through e-mail. By the time your author arrives you'll have developed a professional relationship, they'll have a connection with you, and they'll have a sense of familiarity about your school.

The most essential part of the visit is unequivocally contingent on how well prepared you, your guest, and your audience are. Here are the bare basics:

1. Ask whether the author will have special technology needs for his or her presentation. This prevents the author from having to lug too much equipment.
2. How many sessions does the author fee cover? Two one-hour long presentations? Four separate forty-minute sessions? Figure this out in advance, discuss it with your guest, and then organize class schedules accordingly.
3. Find out the author's preference regarding audience size. Some authors can handle hundreds of students in the auditorium; others are more comfortable with an intimate class size. If you can have a small group, the students' experience will be more memorable. In a journal entry, one of my students candidly wrote, "At my old school it

was boring to meet an author. The author talked to the entire school at once. Not everybody got to ask questions. There wasn't much time. This time (at NCS) the author really wanted us to speak to her and share our thoughts and ideas. The authors at my old school just wanted to get it over with." If you can create an environment in which students can look the author in the eye, ask him or her questions, and be physically close to the author during the presentation, the experience will be meaningful for everyone.

4. Strategize the groupings. Who are your most willingly enthralled and captivated audience? Probably the younger students. Contribute to the success of the day and help your author by having the elementary students at the first presentation. This is a logical way to have your author primed before he or she is faced with the ruthless "come on, make me smile" upper classman.

5. Provide your author with insight into the group. Which stories and books have the students read? How extensively have the titles been covered in the curriculum? Have the author's titles been available at book fairs? Have they been circulated around the faculty and administration? Are there controversies to explore? What issues within the work would the teachers like to have addressed?

6. While working on multicultural literature in our curriculum, the author's life experiences in cultural diversity, notable in their work, were important to discuss. Tie-ins to your curriculum are a must and enhance the standard plot, theme, and structure focus that are typically covered in the classroom.

7. Time for autographing? Don't let this somewhat idle process take time away from your presentations. Have titles piled, with students' names attached on Post-It notes, for the author to work on during down time. Make sure you include titles that you've put aside for gifts: personalized titles for faculty members who were integral in getting the author's work into their classroom, for book club members, and for end-of-the-year reading awards.

8. Have the cash ready. Once again, don't make the author ask for the fee. Have the honorarium check, plus any travel expenses, if possible, ready for the author before he or she leaves.

ADVANCED FACULTY PREPARATION

If you want your author visit to be well received and utilized to the max by your faculty, spend the time to do your best to introduce and prepare them—in advance. Don't make the mistake of assuming they'll know who's coming to visit. Though you realize how fortunate the school is to be hosting your guest, the biggest names in the YA market won't necessarily be recognized by faculty members.

Before Chris Crutcher's visit I did a ProQuest search and e-mailed several of his articles on censorship and diversity to my headmaster, dean of faculty, dean of students, and English department head. I included this note: "We had a successful professional development workshop on diversity during orientation. When Chris visits, should we consider continuing this conversation and ask him to facilitate a diversity session? Is there extra cash available for such a professional development workshop? Let me know your thoughts." They had heard about Chris Crutcher as a big name in the YA author field. Introduction to his professional essays made the administration eager to engage him in our grassroots concerns. It helped to have the support of important members of the administration and it certainly accentuated the excitement over his overall reception.

PREPARING FOR THE VISIT

Don't waste your money or the author's time if you aren't willing to put effort into the details. I've known authors that have walked out on an ill-mannered and ill-prepared school group. Our students and faculty have always been incredibly receptive toward our authors. Writers are people with big imaginations, but they are not necessarily public performers. It's unfair to expect an author to arrive ready to entertain classes with a captivating theatrical performance. Don't set yourself up by having students disappointed by unreasonable expectations. An author's visit is not a show-and-tell, and a well-prepared audience will appreciate the opportunity and gain intellectual rewards from the experience.

The following are the bare basics:

1. Once you and the author have devised a tentative schedule, distribute it far in advance to your faculty. Don't assume anything. Make certain that you post the schedule in a central location in the staff room. Put it on the school's monthly calendar so that special-instruction faculty (music, Hebrew studies, vocal classes, team sports, etc.) will know about the visit. Does it conflict or adversely impact anyone's classes? This may seem like an incidental detail—particularly because *you* will consider the visit the single most important activity of the semester—but other faculty will be occupied with their own agenda. One year our entire 7th grade was preparing to shove off on an all-day canoe trip the day of our author visit. Talk about panic! What a disappointment (to say nothing of the wasted money) this would have been. Advanced planning and discussions will help to avert such scheduling mishaps.

2. Pick apart the author's resume for material that might pique your students' interest. For instance, one of my 4th-graders asked about Tim Wynne-Jones, "Is he famous?" Fame is fickle. This same student considered an older kid that walked around the cafeteria with pencils stuck up his nose heroic. Tim is famous for a literary career that spans four genres: picture books, children's books, young adult works, and adult mysteries. He is the recipient of numerous awards for literary achievements and enjoys a writer's spotlight as a frequent *Horn Book* columnist. Such claims to fame are sure to make a kid yawn. Reviewing Tim's ten-page resume, I discovered that he had also written lyrics for *Fraggle Rock* and had secured *Guinness Book of World Record* notoriety by a reading in front of the world's largest audience of 20,000 with J.K. Rowling. Guess what? My student was starstruck. Do you want to get your students excited about the visit? Then do your homework.

3. Have the visiting author's books been banned? I e-mailed Chris Crutcher with this question and his response was, "Yes. At least one of my books has been banned in every state in the United States—except West Virginia." I want my kids eager to read, and I'll use every tactic I know. I shared Chris's response with students and added, "Don't tell your parents." Talk about guaranteeing a strong readership! I had to hide the library books that the English teachers were planning to use with their classes before they flew off the shelves.

4. Ask your staff what they want the author to cover, and then ask the author to address your faculty's requests in advance of the visit. Keep your faculty's suggestions in the forefront of your correspondence with the author.

5. Draft up single-page information sheets with excerpts from the authors' work, bio blurbs, and reviews. The brevity of the page is essential if you expect busy staff to read it. Circulate the sheets to *every* staff member, your administrators, business officer, nurse, service staff—don't overlook anybody. You never know who may be interested in this event, and you don't want to offend or shut anyone out.

6. Pick apart the author's resume, biographical material, and interviews that you've researched, and put together an in-depth information packet. This should be aimed toward your faculty, allowing them to easily pull information and incorporate it into their classes. They will appreciate and utilize your research.

7. Distribute the information packet to the school's newspaper, newsletter, office, and the community media in advance. This will keep everyone well informed before the event.

PREPARING STUDENTS

First and foremost, integrate the author's material throughout the curriculum so that students have a strong background and familiarity with the literature. A collaborative faculty will be instrumental in establishing this familiarity. Another way to familiarize students with an author's work prior to the visit is to use a Reader's Workshop design (see Reader's Workshop, Chapter 8). Once the author arrives, well-informed students will engage in intelligent, relevant, and meaningful conversations.

Here are the bare basics:

1. Have multiple copies of the author's titles scattered in every nook and cranny of your school. The material will be read in homeroom, ESL, life skills, the nurse's office—leave no space untouched! This is your key to opening the author's work up to everyone.

2. Have enough copies of the titles available for classes to use within their literary circles.

3. Tell kids the irresistible literary trivia that will raise adult eyebrows. My students loved knowing that Chris Crutcher was a proponent of freedom of speech through his advocacy for children's rights. I read students this comment about Chris's title *Whale Talk*, "I'm feeling pretty combative these days because I believe that good stories can lead to great discussions between adults and teenagers and because I believe that stories about hard times can make people in hard times feel less alone."

4. Don't assume that your students will realize what they're about to get. Coach them about the privilege of having an author visit their school. Help them understand that such opportunities are limited experiences.

5. Have some students serve as the author's hosts and let them have lunch with her or him.

6. I hold a literary book club with my older students during their arts elective block. We comb through everything about our visiting author and completely immerse ourselves over and beyond the classroom exposure. These students then attend a special lunch with the author.

7. All of your hard work will contribute toward students being good hosts, listeners, and enthusiastic participants.

8. Have students write down questions for the author in their Reader's Response journals. These pre-composed questions help diminish shyness and serve as the prelude to more impromptu and spirited conversations.

9. Have students who are planning on attending the Writer's Workshop submit their writing samples to their English teacher in advance of the visit. No exceptions. This assures that the serious student is included and keeps attendance at a manageable level.

INTRODUCTIONS AND PRESENTATIONS

Stay sensitive to the reality that even the most seasoned author will need transition time. They may have traveled a long distance, battled a snow storm, have jetlag, just found out that their PowerPoint presentation won't run on your technology—you know those unexpected surprises. They'll need to adjust to the unfamiliar surroundings. Here are some pointers to help reduce unnecessary stress and make their introduction into your community as welcoming and comfortable as possible.

Don't Overlook the Details

1. Encourage them to arrive the evening preceding the event. The morning of the presentation is just too iffy. It doesn't allow for car trouble, inclement weather delays, traffic snarls, or direction snafus.

2. Discuss the accommodations they would prefer; there's a wide spectrum between people who are comfortable in a bed and breakfast and those who prefer the independence and anonymity of hotels.

3. Will they have a car? If not, you'll want them to stay close to the school. The choice of accommodations will be yours.

4. Plan a faculty dinner with the author at a restaurant. Dinner seems like an incidental and frivolous detail, but it serves as a successful ice-breaker. Also, it may be the most quintessential professional involvement that your staff will experience. The author visit revolves completely around the student. Therefore, dinner with the author offers faculty quality time that is impossible to grab elsewhere.

   a. The dinner gathering is a warm welcome for your guest and a perfect way to become introduced to the major players that have embraced his or her work. Include administrators and faculty members who have been instrumental in getting the author's material into their classroom. It is a compliment to show the guest such attention and just plain good manners. As a bonus, the dinner offers staff members an atmosphere that's conducive to casual and comfortable conversation that's rarely possible during school hours.

   b. Fine-tuning for the student presentation. Ideally the dinner will precede the next day's presentation and will allow time to share the collective goals of the group, that is, discussion of what the faculty have highlighted in using the author's work within their classes, particular stories in which the students are well versed, controversial subject matter that staff would like to have discussed (or perhaps, avoided), and recommended material that students have been particularly excited about and that the author should certainly cover. You will have discussed much of this at length through e-mail correspondence, but the dinner allows the rest of your faculty to speak up.

   c. Planning the Professional Development workshops. The dinner also provides time for collective input for this session and to set criteria. This avoids the pitfalls of having a Professional Development workshop that speaks to a professional organization but not to yours. The dinner group tailors the presentation so that it is customized for your school, has clout for your faculty, and ensures that everyone is invested.

   d. Finally, and perhaps most important, the social dinner establishes a natural familiarity and bonding with the author that spreads into the community even before the first presentation. The morning of the event, staff members can comfortably greet and chat with the author as they pass in the hall. The guest will have become part of the community and feel at home.

5. Ask your guest in advance if you may have permission to videotape the presentation. It will be a tape that you'll be able to share with staff for some great teaching techniques, and it will allow students to revisit the performance. A good author's visit gets better the second time around—especially if the video pans around, showing the audience from time to time.

6. Location, location, location. Set up as many sessions as possible. The smaller the group size, the more effective the presentation. This will be contingent on how many sessions that the original author fee covers. Work together on this. Our student body is small (tiny by most standards), so we can host our visit in the library. We create a warm, cozy environment, carting out the tables and bringing in the threadbare oriental carpet for the smaller students to sit at the author's feet, while the older students sit in a semicircle of chairs behind the younger ones.

   While often a necessity, an auditorium presentation will rarely provide the relaxed and comfortable environment so conducive to a memorable visit. Try to fit everybody in the library—even if it requires several separate sessions.

7. Troubleshooting: Being the host of an author visit means that you'll be troubleshooting in more areas than you can ever imagine. Unforeseen occurrences are rarely catastrophic (well, maybe that time it was 20 degrees below zero and the power went down...), but they can be problematic. I know of a librarian who invited Alvin Schwartz to her school. Alvin experienced a slight heart attack and was rushed to the emergency room the night before he was to talk to her school. He actually showed up for the event the next day. These are extreme cases, but believe me, you do need the freedom of range to be running for the adapter for the projector, or greeting the press that arrives thirty minutes early (or late), proctoring the noisy door that incessantly is being opened, or simply getting your guest a glass of water. Don't try to handle the videotaping or take photos. Delegate some of these responsibilities in advance.

Silly as it sounds, you'll need to remind yourself that the author is alive, and that's exactly why you're introducing him or her to your students. Spending lots of attention on details means that you'll be able enjoy the personalized and creative benefits of an author visit.

MAKING IT BETTER NEXT TIME

After your author visit, step back and assess the presentation from an organizational and instructional viewpoint. What might have been done better? You'll always find something that can be improved. Consider this a constructive assessment and remain receptive to bolstering an already exciting program.

1. Keep a record of the highs and lows; this is an annual event that will build upon itself. Each year you'll discover new things to try and areas to tweak.

2. After the visit, have students get out their Reader's Response journal and reflect on their feelings and impressions of the author. It is important to do this soon after the visit, while impressions are fresh and before daily life claims students' attention. If there's anything that will give credence to the relevance of how invaluable the VAP is, the students' feedback will do so.

   Student assessment will often provide you with new ideas. For instance, after reading the students' responses to outdoor wilderness educator, and storyteller James

Bruchac, I realized that I had completely overlooked one of Jim's obvious strengths: the potential for his instruction on the art of storytelling.

One student wrote, "I learned about Jim's way of storytelling. It was very descriptive. He told it from memory and by the way he knew the story. He told us that every story is passed down and you make it your own. He spoke and walked around and looked you in the eye. He did a good impersonation of voices. His stories are based on his stories from his family. Most of his stories are about either animals or monsters. All of his stories have some kind of a moral or lesson in the end." This student was well prepared to consider style, technique, and traditional stories. She also disclosed something that I had overlooked. We had barely discussed the craft of storytelling while preparing for Jim's visit. This student had quietly observed and recognized the inherent skills that Jim possessed. If not for her entry, I might have missed her astute observation. In retrospect, it's clear to see that a Storytelling Workshop would have been an excellent culmination to this author's visit. I've got it in my notes for next year.

3. Circulate a memo to the staff and request that they give you written feedback on their reflections of the visit. Make up an easy-to-complete evaluation form on which they can check off the answers. The simpler it is to fill out, the more likely it will be returned. Include a space for comments. Don't invite suggestions for the following year's author visit—teachers often know a writer that would "love to come to our school" and while they may be a great choice, if you aren't familiar with the author, it's a risk.

4. Take notes during the visit. It's fun to jot down some of the priceless comments that your students make. You may need to write a report to the grantor of funds that helped sponsor the event. Referring to notes will help to rekindle the excitement of the time and translate into your report. Or you may wish to compile a small article for your school's newspaper or newsletter. Drafting student comments into the piece enlivens it, as well as attracts parents' attention. Consider doing a photo page with quotes randomly scattered. The combination of the photos and quotes provides a quick and comprehensive reference sheet of the event for future referral. Digital photos posted on the school's webpage are a great way for parents to view the good time.

DON'T OVERLOOK THE OBVIOUS

ANECDOTAL ASIDE

It took me sixteen years to focus on Jim Bruchac. He lived only an hour-and-a-half away in Saratoga Springs, NY, was married to the great-granddaughter of one of our school's founders, was related through marriage to one of our faculty, and was the son of Joseph Bruchac, a well-known member of the Abenaki nation, prolific author of Native American literature, and regular contributor to *National Geographic*. Jim Bruchac, noted educatorand storyteller of the Native traditions in his own right, seemed too "Adirondack" for me—too much of the same. I was looking for established YA authors with notable names. I wouldn't pay attention. Ambition spawns tunnel vision.

While in the process of submitting a grant application for a multicultural literature program for the following year, my tunnel vision was finally pierced. Around this same time I received an e-mail from Jim with a casual introduction and some available dates for a future author visit. My response? "What's your father doing? Might he be available?" Ambitious programming revealed my lousy manners.

Our grant application was almost complete. We had lined up YA novelist Janet McDonald, who had received the Coretta Scott King/Jon Steptoe best new talent award in 2003. Could we afford a second author of Native American descent? It fit well within the design of our application, and it made sense to further illustrate the cultural distinctions from within our state. I took a risk, and wrote Jim into the grant, helping to balance and strengthen the overall impact of the multicultural literature proposal. We invited Jim—and I kept my fingers crossed that the pending grant would be approved.

To make a long story short, we were awarded the grant and Jim Bruchac "wowed" our library and bridged the cultural and curriculum divide. He did three author/storytelling sessions one day, and he worked with our already developed wilderness survival and Adirondack geography tracking classes the next. Students wrote things like, "I will never consider tracking boring again." Or, "I would trust my life with Jim Bruchac. I wish he was my father or a neighbor." His natural gift for storytelling and his passion for tracking were infectious. He made time to chat with interested faculty members, and plans for his return were discussed.

I wish I could take credit for tracking down this perfect match for our school—I wish I could pretend that it was somebody else who ignored this treasure at our threshold. What was the hard lesson learned? Pay attention, stay observant and receptive, fight your preconceptions, battle blind ambition, and trust in serendipity.

NOTES

1. Janet McDonald, author of the adult memoir *Project Girl*, and YA titles *Spellbound*, *Chill Wind*, *Twist & Turns*, and *Brotherhood*.

2. Carol Plum-Ucci, author of *The Body of Christopher Creed* (New York: Hyperion, 2001) (Printz Honor) and *What Happened to Lani Garver* (San Diego: Harcourt, 2002).

3. Chris Crutcher, author of *The Sledding Hill* (New York: Greenwillow, 2005), *Ironman* (New York: Greenwillow, 1995), *King of the Mild Frontier* (New York: Greenwillow, 2003), *Crazy Horse Electric Game* (New York: Greenwillow, 1987), and many more YA titles.

4. Alison Follos, "Gantos Is Seriously Funny," *Library Media Connection*, Jan. 2005, Vol. 23, Iss. 4, pp. 50–52.

5. Tim Wynne-Jones, author of *Some of the Kinder Planets* (New York: Orchard, 1995), *Boy in the Burning House* (New York: Farrar, Straus, and Giroux, 2001), *A Thief in the House of Memory* (New York: Farrar, Straus, and Giroux, 2005), and many more children's and YA titles.

6. Alison Follos, "Gantos Is Seriously Funny," *Library Media Connection*, Jan. 2005, Vol. 23, Iss. 4, pp. 50–52.

Chapter 11

RAISING CASH
(AKA: BUDGETS R BOGUS)

Budgetary limitations are everybody's concern. In private schools, where parents are paying tuition, it's uncomfortable to ask for money for what should be covered in the day-to-day academic budget. In public schools, where parents are paying school and/or property taxes, the same is true. I have lived in two very different communities; one was an upscale suburban area with real estate and tax figures so high that the teachers were unable to live within the town where they taught. The high school campus sprawled out like a small rural community college; beautiful athletic fields flanked this prime real estate on the outskirts of town. The education of the town's children was sound and secure; passing the school budgets was a priority.

Now, I live in a rural area where most upper-income families are second-home owners who don't live here. Working-class families, families on public assistance, and senior citizens on fixed incomes live side-by-side. Tax increases are everyone's concern. The high school is a splendid old building in the center of town. Students from outlying towns are bused in. There's a hallway that has pictures of all the graduating classes standing on the front steps—from those of my own two children, who graduated in 2000 and 2002, back to the fifteen students who graduated with the class of 1932.

This town is like many small towns across America where tax increases are defeated unless proven to be crucially necessary. Even in these low-to-moderate income towns, community members try to support the school system—to a point. Here the extras that are considered normal in more affluent communities cannot be absorbed in the annual budget. These rural school systems worry over whether they will have enough money in the budget to pay for an unexpected rise in fuel prices, to reach an agreement in teacher salary negotiations, or to replace an old bus. Arts in education, while attractive, are not considered critical budgetary needs. Special library functions and programming in schools hard-pressed to replace classroom textbooks may be considered extra events.

A business manager once informed me that the money I raised from our annual book fair sales, as well as any educational grants received, would be applied to the library's regular budget. That is, everything raised became part of what was already allocated. I had a testy reaction and decided that I would no longer coordinate the book fair, apply for grants, or solicit additional money from our families for any matter whatsoever. It infuriated me to know that efforts to host special events and recruit additional monetary support were absorbed into our daily budget. No way! When I calmed down, I accepted that additional fundraising is a way to help when the overall school budget is strained and in trouble. But it should never lapse into a normal practice. I accepted the tough news that year but fought to regain my annual budget. I articulated the disappointment of having devoted time and attention toward the purpose of securing additional funding, only to have it swallowed up in the budget. This was a one-time experience. Now all additional funding raised is applied toward specific events.

In a perfect world we have as much as we need, and if not, we need only ask for more. In my little world, I've had many school years when I've had to modify, or put a cap on, my "forward-thinking" plans. There are expenses that fall outside the realm of fundraising, like automating your library. From the way everyone in the profession reacted to my effort in that matter, I felt that our library was the last in the United States not to be automated. I'd wanted to automate but convincing my supportive, but environmentally focused and fiscally minded, administration of its necessity had been tough. Though they admired all the slick and sexy benefits, they really wanted to know only one thing: "How much?" It took me several years to grapple with the figures. It's not a simple matter to collect and present estimates for an overhaul that you've yet to experience. However, it's imperative to do so if you expect to convince people who have no knowledge about the project, its purpose, or its potential—and thus, have no interest. Suffice it to say that what's clearly a priority to you may seem a periphery expense to an administration looking at a multi-million-dollar septic system replacement, a new boarding facility, and unprecedented insurance hikes.

After going back to the drawing board again, and again, and still not winning my headmaster's support, I cried. Then I collected myself. I contacted our school library system regional office for assistance in compiling accurate figures for the first-year start-up costs, the second year's expenses, and a five-year projection. It was a fairly unwieldy figure for a little school library with a small population and a small budget. Nonetheless, I did my homework and presented all the information and budgetary figures in black and white. Having the information clearly organized with all the figures out in the open helped gain my headmaster's confidence. While he reviewed the figures and shared with me a gloomy deficit forecast and reminders about the necessary septic system expense, I thought I might have lost again. Then he became very, very quiet while working up figures on his calculator and considering them yet again. This time he decided we'd go for it. Admittedly, it didn't hurt that our school was having its ten-year review by the New York State Association for Independent Schools. There was a librarian on their team and one of their questions was, "When do you plan to automate?"

Have a purpose for your fundraising efforts, whether it's purchasing a special addition (*Reference Library of Black America*), replacing a threadbare and antiquated Newbery collection, contributing toward an unusual equipment purchase, or hosting a special event. It wasn't all that long ago that I had a book fair to raise money to buy an Apple computer—our first. A few years later, our book fair money purchased a CD tower. Today, technology expenses are absorbed into the annual budget. Fundraising can serve to pay for introducing something new. If it's well received and purposeful, it will prove indispensable and justifiably become part of your annual budget.

BOOK FAIRS R US

Your library is the home to the appreciation of the written word. Book shelves, reading tables, study corrals, newspapers and magazines strewn about, bulletin boards heralding the joys of reading or highlighting an upcoming literary event, photographs of authors' visits, and posters of authors, all help to create a literary atmosphere. Hosting a book fair in this environment is a natural. You have the props and you have an audience. You'll just need more books.

You'll also need your community and school families' support to make a fair worthy of the time you expend and to ensure financial success. Drumming up business is instrumental. Four weeks before hosting a book fair, send a detailed letter to inform parents of the reasons for the fundraising event. An obvious, but often overlooked detail, is that families will support the function if they know what the money is for. Send a press release to the local papers containing this same information. Families that can't attend the event may send a check to support the function in their absence.

If fundraising will support an author visit, tell the families all about it. Paint a brief biographical sketch of the author, explain why you're inviting this particular author in for your students, and highlight some of his or her notable titles. To save words (your letter should never exceed one page), download cover images of the author's books. Layout these postage-stamp-size images as a border print flowing down one margin of your letter's page. If the library has recently received a grant allocation, be certain to point this out in your letter. In addition to being newsy and inviting, a parental letter home reinforces the library as an active presence within the school community.

WHO SHOULD SPONSOR YOUR FAIR?

Having a book fair is like running a bookstore for a few days. It's better, because you don't have the headaches of employees, invoices, and expense overhead. You'll need to decide whether to use a national book fair company or a local bookstore.

Some national companies will come in with the titles preselected, jazzy cardboard display cases, promotional material to circulate to parents, discount packages, incentive bonus points, and a percent of the profits that are able to be applied toward free books. Usually the profit is 30 percent of your sales.

A colleague of mine from a public school told me about her experience using a national company. "We host two fairs a year, and they usually last two weeks, with two evening presentations. Students come in during their scheduled library time the first week and browse. Students can use wish lists to write down titles and prices, and bring the lists home for parental approval. The fair is essentially open for business all day, and therefore, it does disrupt library use quite a bit. I think the amount of profit, which makes author visits possible, makes any inconvenience worth it."

"The fair also helps give me a sense of what students are interested in, and lets me look over some of the newly published titles. We are allowed about $100 worth of paperback titles from the fair." The problem sometimes with the big national fairs is the quality of the books and the addition of lots and lots of junk posters, pens, toys, etc. Local bookstores may be unable to extend as high of a discount, but you'll receive a customized and high quality choice of product.

Every time you host a fair you'll learn something new. It's a fine balance between control and flexibility. Though you'll know exactly how everything *should* run for optimal efficiency to match your high standards, the reality is that you will need some assistance. There will be unforeseen discrepancies and unexpected problems. If you have done most of the preparations in advance, and leave yourself some wiggle-room for troubleshooting, there is little that will arise that is insurmountable.

My colleague at the public school continued:

> I have always done most of the work myself, really for selfish reasons, including so that I'll feel "okay" about not sharing the profits with other school groups. I also find doing most of the work is the most reliable way of running things. I had a book fair volunteer group one year and important things, like press releases and other communications, didn't get done. I've realized that I need to be tighter on contacting parents and setting up a volunteer schedule well ahead of time. Then I need to call parents to remind them of their commitment. For instance, once I was caught short with twenty kindergarteners and the volunteer never showed. Fortunately, the teacher was willing to stay and help out.

In the past our school also used a national book fair company, but I experienced many drawbacks. I requested specific titles that never arrived, title selections were limited to isolated publishers, and the preselected stock we received was always a surprise (not necessarily a pleasant one). Sometimes the stock appeared shelf-worn, as though already in attendance at too many traveling book fairs. There was always lots of profiteering junk: pens, posters, bookmarks, and toys that parents shouldn't be subjected to at a school library presentation. We requested that the material arrive in plenty of time to set the fair up. I need at least a couple of days to present the fair in an organized and attractive manner. One year, the truck that was supposed to arrive two days prior to our scheduled fair arrived the afternoon before the fair. Our fair only runs for a day-and-a-half, and I don't have time to absorb or rectify problems of this magnitude. It was a surprise I could have done without. As with the case at the public school, I was fortunate to have a teacher pitch in and help me set up the fair in a marathon team effort.

That late arrival experience pushed me to research other options by which I could exercise more control over arrival and merchandise. We now work with a privately owned bookstore in our region. Our profit margin is a bit lower because they can't offer the same bells and whistles incentives, but the quality, satisfaction, and personal attention is much higher. We promote our fair with confidence and pride. With the combined expertise of the bookstore owners and myself, we offer a top selection of children's literature and young adult (YA) titles that our families won't find anywhere else.

DETAILS R US

Selecting a date to host your fair is an important decision. You want enough extracurricular activities to draw an audience, but not so much that it's overkill.

Guests should not be too overwhelmed to leisurely browse through the books. The balance for maximum exposure is to entice guests to mosey in while taking a break from the other school events. Visitors enjoy the reprieve of a tranquil environment surrounded by books and will be curious about your literary recommendations for their children.

Timing and presentation are key. North Country School's boarding students stay on campus and celebrate Thanksgiving with their families. The school puts on a huge family-style harvest dinner. During a two-day period, we have many of our students' families and their extended families milling about. Parents meet with teachers, there are academic presentations, art displays are set up around the school, special performances and activities are planned, classrooms are spiffed up, and flowers festoon the building. It's quite a holiday event with hundreds of our closest friends and relatives—and the opportune time to host a book fair to a literally captive audience.

Another logistical plus: Because it is Thanksgiving, the sponsoring bookstore is closed. All the profit we make at the book fair is gravy for the store. With Thanksgiving about three weeks before the winter holidays, our fair is well positioned to launch that all-American tradition: holiday shopping. The bookstore has lots of holiday titles available, which eliminates special ordering and accentuates the winter holiday selections. It makes for a strong and viable partnership.

We open the fair a few hours prior to the families' expected arrival—giving the children something to do while eagerly awaiting their guests. Students get a sneak preview and have books put aside until they have their parents in tow. The fair continues throughout the two days of events at the school. The library is a relaxing space for parents to filter in and out of between appointments with teachers and academic presentations, or while waiting for their child to change for dinner. It also provides them with a place to carry on a private conversation tucked away in the stacks. We try to have the fair open for a few additional hours at the end of the school events to allow faculty some time to browse and buy. We extend a partial discount to faculty.

GETTING WHAT YOU WANT

The following suggestions are aimed at coordinating with a regional bookstore. You can adjust them to apply to working with a national book fair organization.

About six to eight weeks prior to the fair, begin the ordering process. Meet with the bookstore owners to review and discuss new titles. If you're going with a national book fair organization, start the communication process through telephone calls. Whether you choose to work with a store or a larger organization, communicate weekly—then several times a week—and order titles until just before the fair. We request titles that are recommended on our school's Title Trek reading list. Though the library holds these Title Trek selections, parents often want to purchase copies for their child's home bookshelves, or as gifts for siblings, friends, and relatives.

We also request plenty of copies of titles by the visiting author(s). Purchasing these books in advance eliminates the potentially draining commercial aspect of an author visit. In the parental information letter, I let parents know that the author's titles will be available at our fair and that the children will have the option of having the book(s) autographed when the author arrives. I advise parents to notify me in advance if they want the author's book put aside for a surprise gift because that process is apt to go awry if we try to do it during the hectic moments of the fair. At the time of purchase, I place a Post-It note with a student's name on it inside each of the author's books.

The bookstore we work with is very knowledgeable about picture books, regional titles, holiday choices, and adult bestsellers. I have a strong children's literature and YA background. I include a significant number of fantasy and science fiction titles, graphic novels, noteworthy comic collections, and Newbery and Printz award winner and honor titles. I also request several favorably reviewed new titles. Unless a staff member has requested them, I skip the series books available in every chain store across the country.

For your book fair, include your students and staff in the book selection process. This is the most important detail in preparing for the fair. If you're going with a national book fair company, give students catalogues and brochures and ask them to write down titles that interest them. Ask staff to jot down titles that they would like included at the fair. Have them give you their wish lists for resources that they would like added to their classrooms. Make your own list for material that you would like to add to the library's collection.

I take a group of students to the local bookstore a few weeks prior to the fair. These students are our Library Key Kids, students who have earned the privilege—through responsible, independent, and self-motivated behavior—of using the library as a study and/or free-reading space without adult supervision. They are the Good Samaritans of library stewardship. They have the additional perk of picking the books for the fair, and later helping to set up the fair. We browse up and down the aisles with pencil and paper jotting down our literary desires. Many overlooked titles are captured during this visit. Students pick titles that they loved when they were little. A teen's eye is discerning, and adults can be blind to what grabs them. The quality of a fair should be impeccable, not sterile. The students and I have a little discussion before our visit to outline two basics: their behavior at the store and appropriate book selections. (i.e., nothing that might cause Grandma to faint, even if it is hidden between the covers!).

Students love helping to choose the books for the fair and they're conscientious about keeping the material fun and respectable—after all, they're thinking about what their siblings and parents will like as they select titles. Have your students understand that this is their school's book fair and they're your professional resource. This position is certain to have your students enthusiastic, invested, and proud to introduce their family to the library. Their involvement is the best advertisement you can have as they talk up their selections throughout the school.

The more selective you are with the material that is at your fair, the more successful the fair will be. Less is always more. You can't possibly do justice to all that's available, so go with what you know. Let the fair reflect your expertise and what you're able to recommend with conviction. Save questionable material for the bookstores. Though your immediate priority is to raise money, sagacious selectivity will generate long-term and far-reaching implications. Your library will be known as a high-quality, dependable, and reliable resource center. Your fair will build a reputation and become avidly anticipated. The books available at the fair should reflect the selective professional standards implicit in your school's library. First and foremost, a school book fair should emphasize high-quality children's and YA titles. A few appropriate adult titles may enter the mix for good reasons: to draw in the dads and the sophisticated students who won't sully their hands with anything reeking of "young", and to bulk up sales. All adult titles should be appropriate reads for young adult readers.

COLOR IT FESTIVE

Remember Martha Stewart? It's wise to keep your decorating under control. Apply your energies toward selecting the best material and organizing your space well, and then let the kids make it festive. Keep a critical eye on the overall presentation.

Our presentation employs a harvest theme, so we use strands of colored leaves (purchased from the Dollar Store) to decorate the room. One of my stylish and sophisticated students told me they look "awful and chintzy." I told her that when she comes up with a better idea, I'll defer to her tastes. Until then, streamers fan out over doorways and balloons dangle from the ceiling. A cautionary note: One year, after spending hours (and extra cash) to set everything to perfection, the morning of the fair greeted me with sagging streamers and deflated helium balloons. Keep it simple. You want browsers to be wowed by the books, not distracted by the decorations.

Origami cranes are a delicate addition that students never tire of making. My students work on the cranes during their Reader's Workshop classes, academic classes; they'll even come in and make them during recess. The cranes pile up all around my desk. Sometimes a new pile will greet me on Monday mornings. When the day comes to decorate for the fair, we thread the cranes and drape them along ceiling beams. Simple and fanciful, they sway in the breeze of an opening door, and if left up long enough, cobwebs attach to them and they seem to dance on their own. It's very cool.

Another easy decorative touch is tissue paper flowers. They look dramatic, are inexpensive, and can easily be created by a noncrafty librarian and a group of kids. They look awesome tucked into vases and last all year.

BE ULTRA-PREPARED

Just like with getting ready for your author visits, it pays to expect the unexpected and be overly prepared for a book fair. Here's an example of why:

Once upon a time I was preparing for my sixteenth Thanksgiving book fair. I should have been able to pull this off by rote habit, but the challenge still sent my adrenaline level soaring. In a few days' time I had a presentation to give to our parents as well as the book fair to set up. Life has this rude habit of disrupting my carefully constructed plans. My two (young) adult children were due home for the Thanksgiving holiday, one from college and the other from Washington, DC. My dog's tail had a sore on the tip of it that hadn't cleared up in four weeks despite several visits to, and frequent telephone consultations with, the vet. Medication, bandages, setbacks, and hundreds of dollars tied up with ineffectual veterinarian advice brought us no further to absolving her discomfort.

On the Friday morning prior to our book fair, I was up at 3:30 a.m. with our dog because she was crazy with pain again and her tail bandage was a bloody, sodden wreck. My husband and I wrestled her down and rebandaged her. By 8:00 a.m. I was on the telephone with the vet. He was out for a walk. I drove to his office only to have him quickly bandage the tail, give her a sedative (I begged), and he nastily chastised me, saying next time I should make an appointment because now he was backed-up for the rest of the day. My poor dog! This time when I cried, I swore.

Then I remembered that the books were arriving for the fair that morning and I was now *really* late for school. The books arrived before I did. I brought my dog into school with me. She became so excited when she saw the kids that she wagged her tail in glee, the bandage flew off, her tail hit the wall, and in an instant she was howling and the library was a spray of blood. Nothing was spared, including the high piles of boxed books. Thankfully they were protected by thick cardboard. I actually said a mini-prayer of thanks that the books were okay in between freaking out about my dog. It wasn't until much later in the day that I noticed my face was sprayed (I looked like I'd been in a fox hunt), and a photograph of my daughter, tacked behind my desk, had some suspicious red speckles on it.

This story could go on for another chapter, but I'll cut to the chase. That Tuesday I had to give the presentation to the visiting parents at our school. It was also the eve before our book fair opened. It also was the day that our new vet told us our dog's tail would have to be amputated. Happy Thanksgiving…Fortunately, in spite of all these unexpected problems, I was so well prepared for the book fair that I pulled it off without a hitch. In fact, it was a record-breaking year. And only my daughter noticed those telltale speckles on her photograph.

The moral of the story: Prepare for the worst. It's wise to have the books arrive a few days before the fair. The library can remain open up until the books are unpacked and put on display. Boxes and boxes will arrive. Have a dolly-cart and some muscle-kids to help unload. We have the boxes arrive late in the afternoon two days prior to the fair and stack them along one side of the room. The mystery of piled-high boxes amplifies excitement throughout the school community. Build upon that. Don't open those boxes! It's tempting, but refrain. Once the boxes are open, they become fair game for curious children (and bloody-tailed dogs). Your school is responsible for the merchandise, so while the library is open, keep the boxes under wraps.

Ask the maintenance staff to carry in some big cafeteria-style tables. Pack up your magazines to free up the magazine rack, box up the paperbacks and videos on the spin-around displays, and generally get your space emptied and prepped to become a bookstore.

Assess your space and how it best lends itself to setting up the fair. Our fiction, magazines, and newspapers are in a round reading room, whereas our research, reference, and nonfiction titles are on the opposite side, in another section. Use the distinct spatial separations to put picture books and children's literature in one area, and YA, adult titles, and nonfiction titles in the other. Regional theme titles, almanacs, dictionaries, DK Eyewitness titles and other nonfiction favorites should be grouped together to draw attention.

Our library's Key Kids help to unpack and organize. Their invested energy and interest drives the success of each book fair. Direct the process, but let the kids do the set-up. Once the students have gone, close the door, and take an hour or so to give it your critical once-over, and spiff it up.

Enlist artistic students to help make signs such as "Newbery Awards," "Mystery," "Young Adult Fiction," "Our School's Recommendations," etc. Organize titles much the way they catch your attention in a store: holiday picture books on countertops, pricey hardcover books displayed on easels, sci-fi and fantasy titles on spin-arounds, and Newbery award recipients grouped together on a table. Your school's reading list should definitely be featured. Create a central display that showcases the titles your school endorses. The better organized the material, the easier it is for parents to find what they need quickly.

Hold a poster contest to advertise and promote the book fair. Our bookstore sponsors gift certificates for the winners. We select an honorable mention poster from every grade to encourage the entire school to enter. The first-place poster is framed and placed in the library. This stirs up student participation. Parents like nothing more than to see their child's art displayed in the hallways. I like nothing more than seeing the "Come to the Book Fair" theme pulsating in original art forms up and down the hallways.

Invite staff members to come in for a preview. Request that they select titles that they would like added to the collection. From their choices create a "Wish List" section, and keep it near the cash box. Parents can then donate the title to the library in their family's name.

Once the fair opens, be available and on the floor to help shoppers, students, and their families. Another staff member or community volunteer who is comfortable working with money should handle sales. This person must be willing to give you a 100 percent commitment and be without other responsibilities during the time that the fair is open. He or she should be able to manage and be responsible for a cash drawer, run charge cards, and, in a private school, coordinate billing for families who wish to charge to their school accounts. I rely on our business manager, who is really the only person aware of whether Mr. John Doe has paid his school account or is delinquent on his child's tuition. Not having to worry about the money allows me the freedom to help shoppers, as well as to keep an eye on the merchandise. It is also helpful to have a student "bagger". This task may be handed-off to a few students throughout the day.

There may be cases in which a student's family is unable to attend the fair. Printed permission forms stating, "Johnny may spend $_____ on books at the school's book fair. Signed, Johnny's Folks" will prevent a student from being left out. Include the form with your PR letter or have it available a week prior to the event. These forms may be e-mailed or faxed in. Verbal consent to the business manager may be accepted over the telephone.

IT'S ALL ABOUT THE CASH

Now, more than at any other time, your professional expertise and knowledge will be on public display. School librarians are a school's best-kept secret. We're usually not part of parent-teacher conferences and PTA meetings, and generally we're not the adjunct staff milling about on the athletic field. Our public visibility is limited. We may be front-and-center at a school board presentation, or give a PowerPoint presentation for faculty on using the next installment of the "federated" online system, but generally, we reach a small and predetermined audience. Take advantage of this wonderful opportunity to interact with the extended families of your students. Your knowledge of children's and YA literature is one of the most valuable assets of the fair. Families will rely on and benefit from your experience. You've guided their children toward good books; offer them the same attention. Families will appreciate your ideas, not only for their child's sake, but also for siblings, cousins, and friends.

A book fair should appeal to and attract the students first, so have the latest Harry Potter available, but don't be cornered by the mass market. Follow your instincts. Strive to host a fair that exceeds the norm and resists superficial commercial trends. Parents will find those titles saturating every bookstore around the country and they'll appreciate that they aren't barraged with them at the school's book fair. It will make the difference between families feeling like they're trapped in a consumer's nightmare, or having a great experience viewing carefully selected literature in a comfortable atmosphere. Give your fair elevated distinction by offering the highest quality material available. Showcase books that have stood the test of time as well as today's top choices. Select titles that families will be proud to give as gifts and that readers will treasure. Share the titles that you have personally felt a connection to over the years. The optimal situation is that you will be able to pick up any title from any table and chat it up with confidence.

Every year after our fair I suffer from delusions of wanting to own a bookstore. Tallying up the sales, I become completely full of myself and want to swoop down and bestow irresistible titles upon lucky customers. Then reality strikes: Once upon a time Ms. Guiding-Know-It-All Librarian (me) was unpacking books to set up my Thanksgiving book fair. I came across a most unusual and enticing title. With a chuckle I showed my coworkers and then tucked it where it would be kept away from judgmental parental eyes. Later that year, the book, Carolyn Mackler's *The Earth, My Butt, and Other Big, Round Things* (Cambridge, MA: Candlewick, 2003) won a 2004 Printz honor medal.

The moral of the story? Stay sensitive toward your audience, but don't insulate them. Don't censure. If you feel something may be offensive, particularly if it is sensational solely for sensationalism's sake, stay true to your sensibilities. Don't deliberately set traps in the way of your best intentions and stir up controversy at the loss of quality. It's your party and you have the liberty to serve up what you're comfortable with and knowledgeable about. Just don't ignore what might be exemplary contemporary material because of a tantalizing title or cover.

The end result of a book fair is that you will sell a lot of books for a good cause, and you'll feel good about it. Monday morning, when the kids are back in class and you're all by yourself packing up those seemingly endless—and heavy—boxes to send back, you'll regain your professional sensibilities. Take another glance at the profit tallies, think about the families that now know what you do, and most of all, think about the student who just stopped in to tell you about "the best book!" that they read over the holiday weekend. It's *worth* it at multiple levels.

BIRTHDAY BOOKS AND READING PROGRAM DONATIONS

A very simple way to expand your book buying power is for families to donate a book to the library in their child's name. This can be a "birthday book" in honor of the student's birthday, or you can connect it to your reading program. We call ours "Top Title Trek Choice."

During the summer I send out a letter to all of our students' families. I use this letter as an opportunity to inform parents about our reading program as well as our book donation program. I include a list of the selections from the previous year. This gives parents a concrete example of the quality of the titles that are being added to the collection directly from their support. I also invite families to suggest titles that their child likes, or to recommend a magazine subscription that we may not hold. It is made clear that though we appreciate their input, the final decision is ours. On the bottom of the letter there is a return form for them to sign and send back with their check. The amount we charge for each book is $16. This year I had one family write that their child could select twenty titles!

In order to make students an active part of the program, include them in the process. We place our big orders twice a year. When the new books arrive I put them out on display all around the library's tables. I announce at a council, or whole-school assembly, that a new shipment has arrived and students should come in and select their titles. Frequently there are purchases made with a particular staff member and/or student in mind. In those cases, I'll make personal contact, saying something like, "Sam, the new Anthony Horowitz book has arrived. Looks like a good one."

When a child has selected a title, we place a bookplate in the front of the book with:

> This book was
> Donated to the NCS library
> In honor of Xia Xander's Birthday.
> *November 1, 2005*
> It comes highly recommended!

Xia is given the privilege of being the first reader able to sign the title out. When a student spends the time to select their book donation, it's nice to have a spine label that quickly identifies the book as part of this special program. Graduates will return and look for their donation on the shelf. A spine label helps to locate them.

In the event that a student's family is unable to support the program, or simply chooses not to contribute, I let the child select a title if they're interested. In my mind, we purchase books with or without the parent's additional endorsement, so why leave a child out?

TOP TITLE TREK CHOICE

We've kept the above birthday book model in mind, but we also expanded the premise of donating books to our reading incentive program, Title Trekking. We ask students to recommend a title that they have been looking forward to reading, that their friends would like to read, and that they feel would be a great addition to the Title Trek reading list.

We compose our new Title Trek list and include many of their choices. Then we print a Top Title Trek list, including the student's name next to his or her selection, to share with the parents. Some years we create a list composed exclusively of these titles.

Public school libraries may choose to promote this program more subtly, as parents may feel that they pay school taxes and object to being hit with yet another financial request. Within all your correspondence, you should make families comfortable with the knowledge that these are voluntary programs.

STRETCHING THE FUNDS

As I mentioned in the beginning of this chapter, budgetary concerns are different in different school systems. If you're in a situation in which improving the quality of your library program is limited by budget constraints, remember that you can take the initiative to change this. As with anything in life, nobody is going to come knocking on your door with a pot of gold just because you need it. You'll need to propose your intent and prove the direct benefits.

With every aspect in the library profession, your best strategy is being overly, and maybe overtly, organized. Attending to details means proposing a sound representation of your needs: This greatly helps to legitimize your request.

Here are some suggestions to contend with budgetary woes:

1. Propose an itemized budget to submit to your administrator and business manager of what the library's needs are for the following year(s). Keep in mind that though all departments are asked to do this, many don't, while others do a mediocre job. Apply attention toward presenting a clear and precise document. Include the following items:

   • New and/or replacement of technology: computers, printers, fax machines, copiers, and/or scanners. Subtotal each individual item and then have a grand total. Itemizing the equipment may mean that you'll get some, if not all, your equipment needs.

   • A quote for your annual magazine subscriptions

   • A quote for newspaper subscriptions

   • A quote for the database subscription. Itemize the annual fee for individual databases and sum the grand total; again, you may get some, if not all, of the requested databases.

   • An estimated book budget

   • Any unusual (expensive) reference purchases. Will you need to order a new encyclopedia(s)?

   • An estimate of supplies: book processing as well as special art supplies for students in-class use

   • Automation equipment

   • Automation annual expenses

   • A projection of the Visiting Author Program costs: honorarium, travel expense, lodging, and dining

   • Postage: consider interlibrary loan growth and informative letters to parents regarding the upcoming book fair, author visit, and "thanks for the support letter"—these all make postage estimates an important figure to include.

2. Stretch your special events budget by teaming up with other departments. This is such an obvious and logical solution; it surprises me how often it's overlooked. Take time to chat with the dean of faculty, department heads, and anyone else who may have an

overview of the whole curriculum. This is where curriculum maps are particularly helpful.

When I scheduled a storyteller, we collaborated with other departments to help with the expenses. That year we had a wilderness survival unit in our 6th-grade class while in the 7th grade, they were studying Adirondack geography. We were fortunate to bring in a regional storyteller who was also a wilderness/environmental educator. It was natural to invite him for the library's Visiting Author Program and then split his day (and fees) with the other classes. I coordinated the events, the schedule, and his accommodations. Faculty members were delighted not to have to deal with the details. Combining budgets will stretch funds further, initiate enhanced collaborative programming, and enable you to offer guest artists attractive and realistic honorariums.

3. Stretch your special events budget by teaming up with other schools. This requires more of a concerted effort toward planning and arrangements, but it's certainly feasible. I've done it several times, and I will do so again next year. Not only does it stretch your budget, it also extends your collaborative circle. Teaming up with professionals outside of your school strengthens your chance to achieve collective goals. Exchanging experiences, and learning how other librarians have organized their event or solved troublesome problems, is one of the best ways to perfect your program. Having the chance to work and brainstorm with colleagues within your field is personally rewarding and invigorating. It's continuing education in its most expressive state.

4. Next to your administration's endorsement, the most effective sources of funds are probably outright grants. Pursue arts and educational organizations. If there's a teacher's center, contact it to find out about regional sponsors. Also, your library system office will have information on available grants within your area. Use the Internet to locate agencies that offer grants that support reading, reading programs, and libraries.

5. Some states' educational web pages will post information about available grants and/or links to other sources. New York State's Library Association offers numerous links to grant resources and, in partnership with GrantStation, brings readers the *GrantStation Insider* each week. The *GrantStation Insider* provides subscribers with the latest information on new funding programs, upcoming grant deadlines, conferences, and trainings, as well as relevant information for grant seekers. The opportunities covered are available to those in the New York State region, but GrantStation also showcases national events and organizations (see http://GrantStation.com).

GRANT WRITING

When you've located a possible grantor, request a copy of their application. Before you get started, look over the entire application carefully. Read the fine print, and if need be, place a call to the organization to discuss any questions that you have. Check the application deadline and give yourself a realistic chunk of time to complete the grant. It is worth doing this preliminary footwork to adequately research the grant and find out if your proposal is within its guidelines. You'll find grant administrators very helpful. They are in the same bind as you are: too much to read, too little time. They would rather not review grant applications that don't fit their criteria.

Don't let the application intimidate you. Because I'm paranoid, I figure that grantors want you to be intimidated so that you won't apply. That way they won't have as many applications to read. As daunting as the form may appear, remember that it looks that way to everybody. Few of us approach a grant application with excitement. It's important to concentrate on this: The grant will be awarded. If you don't apply, it certainly won't be awarded to you.

Take a breath and sit down in a quiet place where you won't be disturbed. Distractions are a kiss of death for grant applications—especially because you'll pray to be interrupted, you'll want to be distracted, and you'll embrace any excuse to procrastinate. I've even considered taking up smoking again, just to have something else to do. Focus and settle in.

As I tell my students in our Title Trek reading program, the most difficult part will be to start. Ignore those piles at your desk, e-mail, the telephone, the needy dog begging for a walk, and in my case, even the vacuum—that's just how easy it is to pull me away from grant writing. Fill out the application to the best of your ability. Admittedly, there have been times when a grant application has spent the weekend with me. The tradeoff is that if our school is awarded the grant, a newly designed program, funded for the first year, is destined to become a creative addition to the curriculum. Often a grant allows a pilot program to evolve into a permanent one.

Completing a grant application turns ideas into action. It takes the skeleton of an outline proposal and fleshes it out into a full-fledged program design. Last year I filled out a grant application, drawing from bits of past programs, and structured the beginning of a new integrated curriculum design for the following year. Okay, so sometimes it seems like you're "making it up as you go." Actually, you're sitting down and formulating innovative ideas that have been kicking around in your head and have gone nowhere. Completing a grant application will develop an organized project and give structure to what was a fleeting, random notion. Even if you're not awarded the grant, you'll undoubtedly use the draft, refining and redefining it so that it fits within your prescribed budget.

Author visits are a desirable activity for grantors to fund. It's worth the research and writing time invested toward this end. Your school is likely to receive the grant. When we were awarded $2,500 to apply toward the Visiting Author Program, it was well worth the time spent. Not only did we have a great pilot program, it was so successful that our school committed an annual budget to fund future Visiting Author Programs. If you don't nab the award, you'll certainly use the curriculum design at a future date, and it may become the pilot program to use when you're ready to reapply, or when you find another grant for which the program is tailor-made.

If you're fortunate enough to have access to people with grant-writing experience, ask them if they would review your proposal prior to submission. Don't subject yourself to too many reviewers. Everyone will have differing opinions, and if you rewrite because of every suggestion you'll never get the application sent out.

As with every suggestion and design that has been presented throughout this book, you'll customize the ideas that fit. You won't do everything all of the time or in one year. You'll use what seems most logical to introduce into your school. You'll pace yourself so that your plans will take root and you won't burn out.

Chapter 12

YOUNG ADULT LITERATURE TO GRAB ADULTS

Harry Potter's *real* magic is that he initiated conversations between students and adults about books. Harry captured kids' and adults' attention and opened a new channel of conversation between children and their parents and teachers, with the current flowing all ways. For librarians, it was the welcomed steppingstone to sharing young adult (YA) fantasy titles with kid and adult appeal, like Philip Pullman's phenomenal Dark Materials Trilogy, *The Golden Compass* (New York: Alfred A. Knopf, 1996), *Subtle Knife* (New York: Random House, 1997), and *The Amber Spyglass* (New York: Alfred A. Knopf, 2000), or Garth Nix's "Abhorsen" trilogy that begins in the netherworld of *Sabriel* (New York: HarperCollins, 1995). Magically and miraculously, Harry shrank the generation gap that widens from 4th grade through high school.

An almost inevitable schism happens after elementary school between adults and children. There's a definite rift in communication. From my vantage point, glaring through this mishmash of miscommunication is the loss of adult interest in children's and teenage literature. There's a certain irony here. Teens are willing and eager to read adult books, bestsellers off their family's bookshelves or their favorite teacher's favorite book. But adults, though anxious over "why our kids won't read," hardly know the titles of today's most popular and compelling YA books.

The adult population pays attention to teen literature when a controversial novel is being used in an English class, or a censoring issue materializes in the school's library. Then well-meaning parents are up in arms, attending school board meetings, alerting an ill-informed public to out-of-context segments of the maligned novel. Banning books and challenging lesson plans are sure ways of getting everyone's attention, but it's an unfair way to judge contemporary literature. Such skewed interest serves to stir a misguided pot of community righteousness. Furthermore, it successfully alienates parents, educators, and students, widening the gap on literary acceptance almost irreparably. Other than this flawed and magnified sensationalized exception, adult knowledge and/or interest in YA books and authors seems nonexistent.

Parents spend enjoyable hours reading with their preschool-age children; elementary teachers devote a part of each day to teaching reading and story time. But what happens to the literature that kids are reading when they get to middle and high school? Very little. Scheduled read-alouds decline or cease to exist, and parents' and educators' familiarity with contemporary YA titles plummets. The literature mainstays of many secondary school classrooms continues to be: *Catcher in the Rye* (Boston: Little, Brown, 1951), *To Kill a Mockingbird* (London: Heinemann, 1960), *Lord of the Flies* (London: Heinemann, 1960), and still a biggie, Ray Bradbury's *Fahrenheit 451* (New York: Ballantine, 1953). Many, many moons ago *my* English teachers used these same novels. Are educators complacently saying that little else of any literary merit has been written for young adults in over thirty years? Such stilted sentiment is like suggesting that the *New Yorker* continue to reprint E.B. White essays because they haven't noticed anything new that's come close.

A LIGHT IN THE SHADOWS

School librarians can educate teachers and parents to become familiar with authors beyond J.D. Salinger, Harper Lee, S.E. Hinton, and Robert Cormier. These authors pioneered a barren territory to define today's rich YA genre. There are many more contemporary writers deserving of inclusion in English departments' array of dependable literary choices. If teachers don't know what's new, they can't break their reliance on has-been, done-that selections. That's why a YA reading program for adults is essential. It will turn the tide from habitual reliance to exciting discovery.

BECOME PART OF THE SOLUTION

Four years ago we broadened our reading incentive program to encourage teachers' participation. Our Title Trek reading program became a whole-school event. It wasn't love at first sight, but it gained winning appeal as I kept plugging the books most likely to raise the consciousness, eyebrows, hackles, and overall interest of our staff.

Obviously, one of the most important ways to hook adults on YA literature is to choose titles that leave no room for error: titles in which the author doesn't fool around with trite or trendy language, contrived themes, or rambling plotlines. If the story isn't riveting from the first few pages, forget about it. Your faculty hasn't the time or inclination. Most YA titles can be read in a few evenings; they're books that can be put down and picked up without losing their flow and that have storylines that pulse with energy. Many have themes that delve into the angst we're so quick to cover up as we *grow up*. After I warned one of my faculty members about a chilling psychopathic character and many diabolical situations in Chris Crutcher's *Chinese Handcuffs* (New York: Greenwillow, 1989), saying that it had nearly done *me* in, she said, "Are you kidding? That's the stuff that got me reading as a kid! Where is it?" So don't make presumptions. Adults will react—not always favorably, but they'll react—and they'll come looking for more.

The YA genre is one that is stimulating and challenging. YA titles wipe away the comfortable distance of age and hit nerves and recollections that are real and poignant. Teens won't suffer a slow-moving plot or a condescending tone. Don't waste their time. They want action-packed material delivered with integrity, credibility, and a punch. They've already stumbled through a multitude of compromising experiences: It's reassuring to read about other kids who have also screwed up. They want to be smacked with the truth, the more outrageous and humiliating the better. For the adult reader who's bringing personal memories to the story, revisiting the drama may be cathartic. Nostalgia sifts through, clinging like dust in an hourglass.

The less grown-ups know about YA literature, the less their children will know. It's my opinion that now, perhaps more than at any other time in history, young adult literature is right-on for today's adolescents. In their still-formative teen years, this is the material that helps them peer through a virtual spyglass and become deeply involved while staying safely distant. Somehow, almost through happenstance, some students do fall into these books. But far too many others will never know they exist. Young adult literature is profoundly powerful—it's important for adults to give it a chance. Becoming part of the solution is what we can do.

JUST SAY YES!

The label "young adult literature" has negative connotations; many kids don't want to be called "young" or be associated with "adults". Additionally, using a YA label limits this dynamic and expressive genre to an inordinately small audience: Adult readers won't browse YA titles. We all know labels matter to teens, but they also matter to adults. If nothing else, they steer people in a specific direction. Dispelling the aura of bad labeling takes effort and action.

The national consensus is that kids and adults are reading less. We know that if adults are reading, they're reading adult titles. School librarians have limited contact with the general adult public, but there's no denying that we have access to adult faculty members—should we choose to.

The school librarian is most productive when disseminating information into our school community. If we collect, hoard, control, and protect information, it serves no purpose. Sharing our knowledge empowers the faculty. Entrusting other capable adults to popularize books with children compounds the power of literature in our students' lives. Faculty members who are aware of the value and literary merit of YA titles will enlighten their students with this gift. I recently gave a presentation to our students' parents. I had to acknowledge this simple fact: As the librarian, I can order the books and design programs, but it's the community that popularizes reading.

As school librarians, we need to stop lecturing kids to read and begin encouraging adults to read YA books. We have the knowledge, the materials, and the ability to forge a love of reading, whether a person is 4 or 44. We need adult reinforcements to discuss books with children over meals, car rides to and from the sports field, interludes in classroom discussion, in the halls—anywhere and everywhere. Building a channel of communication with the adult educators in your school is the beginning. I liken it to a phone tree. Get your faculty involved and they'll get the word out. The party line will spread to other faculty members, to students, and to their parents. Get the science and history teachers engaged, and let the buzz spread down the halls and wash out into the community. When the athletic department begins to pay attention, you can turn your attention back to your daily duties, because you'll have a runaway program. With the exception of our insatiable readers, what reluctant reader isn't apt to try a book recommended by their basketball coach before trying one recommended by the librarian? Talk about dumping labels.

ADULTS SHOULD KNOW

Books marketed for the YA audience do not necessarily begin with that as an intention in the author's mind. They are simply very well told stories that happen to have a teenager as the major protagonist. On the flip side, many adult titles are excellent reads for teens, like Sue Monk Kidds's *Secret Life of Bees* (New York: Viking, 2002), Fanny Flagg's *Daisy Fay and the Miracle Man* (New York: Warner, 1992), Haven Kimmel's *A Girl Named Zippy* (New York: Doubleday, 2001), and Howard Frank Mosher's *Northern Borders* (New York: Doubleday, 1994), to name four off the top of my head. Teen characters are great companions to hang out with. They're daring, fresh, troubled, sensitive, passionate, risk-taking, dogged, and devoted. They're driven by action, intense relationships, diversion, perversion, danger, romance, heart-wrenching pain, and soul-searching introspection. How much more can an adult cope with in a single read?!

Today's Printz Award and honor titles are prime examples of choice YA selections that will challenge adults and pique their interest. Publishers target school librarians, bookstores, and distributors. School librarians, in turn, target students. Students are secretive; if it's a gritty sure-to-be-hidden book, they won't mention it to adults. Adults need to be brought into the circle. Librarians must help. If not for the school librarian, how will adults learn about contemporary YA novels?

RELUCTANT ADULTS

The way to successfully create adult awareness of, and an eventual affinity toward, YA literature, is *programming*. Adults thrive on routine and structure, so programming is essential to engaging their participation. Your investment will require stamina, conviction, and patience, but the payoff is immense.

Every school has its own idiosyncrasies. Step back and assess yours. For instance, North Country School, a junior boarding and farm school in the heart of the Adirondack high peaks, is known for many things, including resiliency, hiking, and an outdoor education program—in short, everything hearty under the sun, from farm chores in the dead of winter to tapping maple trees in the spring. Life is jam-packed, and wedging books into someone's harried schedule can be risky business. Sensitivity toward the faculty's demands is always a prime concern. I looked over the rigorous daily schedule and purposefully, but slowly, began a plan.

You're the person most able to size up your school's calendar, your faculty's pace, and when it's best to launch something new. Conversations with your administrators are essential and will influence your planning. Your administrators should be your strongest advocates.

To bring adult readers into the YA literary arena, do your homework. Read everything you can get your hands on. Read a large pool of the award winners, but don't neglect your personal preferences. Teachers will trust your expertise and recommendations. The more invested your staff become, the more they'll rely on your suggestions. Once they're involved, they'll channel a steady flow of books into their classes. With the faculty increasingly well versed and knowledgeable about children's and YA literature, students will read more. This is the message that your administration must hear loud and clear.

GETTING THE BIG GUYS GOING

Faculty members establish a social structure much like that of teens. Trying to have them voluntarily embrace a reading program can be dicey. They already have gobs of schoolwork to deal with, they are into the swing of their own curriculums (or running to catch up), and, quite frankly, they're overwrought with getting reports out and setting up conference meetings with parents—and, oh yeah, they may also have a life. They're probably not eager to jump on your bandwagon. Wooing the faculty might feel as precarious for a shy and introverted librarian as trying to entertain a Las Vegas crowd. The bottom line is that your faculty's participation is an integral component of the overall plan to get students to read. So take a deep breath and hit the stage. You know why, and here's how:

The Administrative Element

- Meet with your administrator and discuss strategic guidelines. Have a written plan ready to present that outlines how the program will be implemented. Have several copies available to distribute to key members of the administrative staff: the guidance counselors, development departments, and certainly the business manager. Exercise time-management skills by assessing the school calendar in advance. Is September a time when changes are disruptive or when new ideas will be comfortably accepted? Perhaps the end of the school year works best. Or would winter or spring break be the time to introduce something new? Let the administration know that you've considered the tempo and the most opportune time to implement successful new programming.

- A sure way to have the faculty sample this new program is to recommend to your administrator to have faculty members read a YA or children's title over the summer. (Okay, yes, now it's an assignment.) Instead of requiring staff to read one or two pedagogical works by "today's educators" (excluding this one), convince administrators to give teachers a break by offering up a YA read. Remind your administrators that staff members will return to school armed with some new YA material to spark up the classroom curriculum.

- Within your program outline, include time slots allocated during spring and/or fall meetings to hold informal literary circles and booktalks.

- It cannot be reiterated enough: Highlight the potential for this material to be *integrated into the classroom*. Administrators must understand the importance of this. It will transform their school from a nonreading zone to a contemporary hotbed of children's and YA literary energy. Our faculty is knowledgeable about children's and YA literature because they read these books. They comfortably have conversations about new titles with their students. They recommend titles to students who don't consider me their best resource. Most importantly, they use these books in their classes. At lunch time I can't get a 4th-grade boy to stop putting grapes up his nose, but the influence of a rad-dude teacher gets him to read.

BOOKTALKS AND COMMUNICATION

- Tempt adults toward children's and young adult titles gently. Adults can be a suspicious lot, and they'll balk at a heavy-handed sales pitch. We launch our YA booktalks in the spring and promote our newest sure-thing titles.

- A spring booktalk session is the optimal time to introduce the following year's visiting author and have their titles available. Six months is not too far in advance for faculty to become familiar with an author's work. That way they'll be able to most effectively integrate the author's work into their fall curriculum.

- Present a young adult literature program to your staff at an opportune point in the year. I find that spring works well; with summer vacation on the horizon, faculty members feel hopeful and are willing to try something new. Introduce the YA reading program to adults at least six weeks prior to a school break. This provides ample time to talk up "the perfect book" to teachers dragging their feet and griping, "All right, what do I have to read?" It also allows time for staff to come in and browse the collection during their free time.

- Offer to present staff booktalks twice a year. Talks before the fall and summer faculty meetings work well at our school. Prepare mini-booktalks in advance. Write up your blurb on an index card. Try not to exceed five sentences. Tape the cards to the book backs for quick reference while you hold the book up for display; use approximately twelve separate titles pulled from vastly different styles. This takes about thirty minutes to present.

- Print your booktalks into a mini-annotated list. Have copies for your faculty members to refer to. This gives faculty a reference to make notations on and check off titles that they are particularly interested in following up on, and it provides them with a reminder to come back later for books that they may not be ready to take out.

- Keep booktalks brief: Never go on and on, or you'll lose your audience. If your audience begs to hear more, don't give in. If it's before summer vacation, talk (even yours) is the kiss of death for teachers eager to get out of school. Whet their appetites and then say, "Read the book." They'll want to read the hot new titles, so plan to begin waiting lists. If funds are available, consider ordering duplicate copies. I've requested money from the professional development budget to meet this need.

- After your booktalks, showcase new titles and save time for browsing. Have the displayed books sorted into categories such as: young adult issues, fantasy/science fiction, historical and realistic fiction, romance, suspense, graphic novels, autobiographical, underground edgy reads that kids love and adults worry about, and children's titles for specific grades. This makes it efficient for faculty to quickly locate their interests.

- Invite parents in for an after-school children's and YA booktalk session. Model it after the faculty presentation above. Carefully assess your school's calendar and select the best time for maximum attendance. Run a brief workshop during an open house evening? Hold a presentation prior to an upcoming school book fair? Use your ingenuity, but certainly include the families.

- Direct department heads toward titles that fit their curriculum areas. Coaches will appreciate Chris Crutcher's *Stotan!* (New York: Greenwillow, 1986) and *Ironman* (New York: Greenwillow, 1995), Robert Lipstye's *The Contender* (New York: Harper & Row, 1967), or Tessa Duder's *In Lane Six Alex Archer* (New Zealand: Oxford UP, 1987).

- Select highly readable material. Use the same logic (and your librarian's sixth sense) that you use with your students. Match the book with the personality. Choose books to enjoy, mull over, talk about, and ultimately, prompt readers to come looking for more.

- Listen for and respect faculty recommendations. Ask staff to share their favorite YA titles with you. Their contributions may be adult novels with teens as the main characters. This is okay and inspires conversation. If you're comfortable with their suggestions, consider adding them to the recommended reading list. I rarely get out of my children's and YA realm, so I appreciate being informed of adult books suitable for young adults. A shared faculty recommendation is how I discovered Pete Hamill's powerful and evocative *Snow in August* (Boston: Little, Brown, 1997). Other adult recommendations we've used are *It's Not about the Bike* by Lance Armstrong (New

York: Berkley, 2001), Robert Olshan's *Clara's Heart* (New York: Arbor House, 1985), and *The Curious Incident of the Dog in the Night-time* by Mark Haddon (New York: Doubleday, 2003).

- Offer guidelines for staff to use in coming up with their choices. George Orwell's *Animal Farm* (New York: Harcourt, Brace, 1954) has become widely accepted and used in English literature and humanity courses. Do we want to recommend something that is already used so frequently? If it's not specifically a YA title (a call that the publishers make), does the book have literary merit, interest, and social significance for today's student audience? What great fodder for discussions! Criteria might include:
  - Are teens the main characters?
  - Are teen issues focal points?
  - Is the subject matter teen-driven and teen-controlled?
  - Does the theme carry an adult sentiment that is overbearing?
  - Is the story being told through a child's and/or teenager's perspective?
  - Is the social climate something that students can relate to?
  - Is the social culture something that will challenge students?

At the end of the school year, encourage staff members to check out one to five books each. They'll chat among themselves about trading books. They'll sell one another on must-read books. The momentum comes from within, and the energy generated by the books in their hands creates a chain reaction.

Some staff members won't bother to peruse the selections and ask, "Okay, what should I read?" Others may pluck a book from the table with a "let's get the heck out of here" attitude. Don't take it personally. No matter how disgruntled they may act, if they leave with a book in their hands your energy was well spent.

Keep your eye out for new recruits. Put a reading list, bookmark, and/or bumper sticker advertising the program into hesitant staff members' mailboxes. Your overture may be just the welcome they need.

For the support and endorsement of your coworkers' participation, extend special thanks. At the end of the school year tuck a bottle of wine, an autographed copy of a book from the visiting author, or a gift certificate to the local bookstore into the mailboxes of staff members who have been enthusiastic participants. Like I've said before, adults aren't all that different from teens: Staff members remind me, "Alison, it's all about the awards!" Their advocacy spreads the word to students, a contribution of immeasurable value. So keep the spirit high and rewards plentiful.

JOURNALING

Investing personal time in any program increases its success. North Country School's reading incentive program, Title Trekking, has soared because students engage in a written dialogue about the books they're reading. Title Trekking encourages students to read books from a carefully selected reading list and reflect about them in their Title Trek journal (see Title Trekking, Chapter 7). Students keep a literary log of the books that they've read. You can encourage staff to do the same.

Your faculty's biggest obstacle will be their concerns about your expectations for their written entry. Teachers can be self-conscious and uncomfortable about submitting their written responses. Allaying their fears of being judged is a good start. Here's what I tell them, "Use this journal as your personal literary diary. Write a bit about the plot, but concentrate on how the book affected you and made you feel. Ten years from now, you should be able to look at your journal and have your entry trigger a personal recollection of the story. Write down quotes that are indicative of the author's style, or that were meaningful to you and you would like to remember." Remind faculty that they are compiling their own annotated bibliography for future classroom reference. That's a wealth of information. I recently heard from a woman who left our school many years ago. She still refers to her journal.

Teachers will entrust their journals to you, and they'll anticipate your reaction. Give them the same intellectual attention that you give your students. Literary journals work well because faculty can reflect upon books during their own time, and you, in turn, can take their journals home, on a plane or a train, to conferences, even on vacation (not recommended—extra weight and you need a vacation). Some responses will prompt heartfelt written dialogues; others may simply require a one-line reaction. Teachers love stickers—use them freely.

Encourage staff members who are involved in the program to take on some of the journal dialogues with the students. Freeing up your control over the journals allows students to expand their literary reflections and conversations beyond the librarian, and it helps to balance the workload. (Don't get too excited here—most teachers aren't banging down the door to take this on, but a few will). It's a good opportunity to collaborate. For schools with a large student population, sharing journal reading and response may be the *only* way to make the journal process happen.

REAL MEN WANTED

The discrepancy between male and female students in ability and desire to read continues to grow. Michael Sullivan, author of *Connecting Boys with Books*, documents, "The National Assessment of Educational Progress (NAEP) reported that not only do fourth-grade girls score higher in reading than boys, but the gap increased between 1998 and 2000. The United States Department of Education statistics show that boys are an average of one and a half grades behind in reading. Boys are two to three times more likely than girls to be diagnosed with a reading disability, depending on different definitions and methods of diagnosis."[1] He goes on to point out the obvious (though frequently and conveniently overlooked) fact that boys lack role models: "Most of all, they don't see men read."

If the male faculty in your school are visibly reading, you're taking steps to dispel the myth that men don't read. My own daughter, now an adult, recently admitted, "I always thought that Dad was illiterate because I only saw him read the newspaper; he never read to me at bedtime and I never saw him sit down to read a book." Ouch. In my daughter's young mind, perusing the newspaper wasn't reading.

Getting adults reading YA titles is beneficial in all of the areas already highlighted: curriculum enhancement, literature integration into curricula areas, professional awareness, and engagement. But getting males involved will have direct consequences upon your male students—particularly because most elementary and middle school librarians are female.

After attending a conference of children's librarians where he was the lone male librarian in a group of two hundred, Michael Sullivan observed:

> In any case, the predominance of women in the field of children's librarianship was clearly highlighted. Women made up 83.4 percent of the profession in the United States in 1998, and the few men in the field experience what sociologist Christine Williams calls the "glass escalator," meaning they are pressured into administrative roles. That leaves few men to do children's work. In more than a decade in the profession, I have actually met only one other active male children's librarian, though I have met a male library director who does children's work and a few male directors who have children's backgrounds. The sum is miniscule. Men simply do not do children's work in public libraries or in elementary school media centers. When most children think of librarians, they think of women.[2]

Male faculty participation in any reading program will help to shift a boy's conception of reading from being a female-dominated, overly literary, sedentary, boring and girly pursuit, to an appealing, male-approved activity. I'm not suggesting macho attitudes; it's more about learning how boys relax and constructively spend their leisure time. When the gurus of education decided it was time to do something about girls' learning problems in math and science, did they pump girls with steroids to make them more assertive and build up their confidence? No, they changed their teaching strategies and reassessed their instructional practices. Similar evaluation and consideration must be given to the way males are being educated. Sedatives are not the answer. Male role models and creative activity might be.

ACTION, READING, AND MALE LEADERSHIP

Men make a literature program exciting. Let them share the program, and help them to realize that their creative energy will provide the shot in the arm to get kids reading. Collaborating with male staff has wondrous results. For instance, whereas I chose to promote reading during the doldrums of winter through a cozy tea-time after-school book club, a male staffer chose a more assertive approach. He challenged students to a grueling combo readathon/ironman event. This was *his* idea of a good time.

The weekend before our Thanksgiving book fair he launched a Triple Trek weekend activity. I noticed that only boys signed up. The point is that they did sign up. Students trekked a mountain, read a Title Trek, wrote about it in their journals, and then watched an episode of *Star Trek*. Prior to the event the teacher commented, "If we have the time, maybe we'll also ride a Trek bike—so it could be a quadruple trek!" They rode the bike, took it apart, carried it up to the top of the mountain, and reassembled it. Boys being boys, they took a picture of it for proof and posterity. Here was male ingenuity at its peak, literally and figuratively.

The Triple Trek began at 6:00 a.m. and concluded at 8:30 p.m.—fourteen-and-a-half hours later! On Monday morning journals were on my desk and the students were proudly complaining about how hard it had been and how tired they were. Males are into grit, brawn, and competition. Everything about the Triple Trek—meshing reading with activity—psyched up our male students. Many boys became new Title Trekkers that weekend.

In preparation for the event, we collected books with "trek" in the title or books about outdoor adventures, climbing, biking, sailing, athletic pursuits, and exploring—and there are lots. We snuck in a few quick reads for students new to Title Trekking. Jack Gantos was visiting later in the year and his Jack Henry books (personal treks) fit the bill.

The Triple Trek activity was completely successful due to the energy from this male teacher. He had invested in the reading program over the summer, having written journal entries on twenty-nine YA and children's titles. He promoted the reading program within his classroom, using several of the titles that he had read the previous summer. Then he organized a stimulating weekend activity pivoting around Title Trekking. Does collaboration get any better?

SEX, DRUGS, AND ROCK CLIMBING

Now that I have your attention...if male teachers were not readers as children, becoming adults, or teachers, will not automatically make them so. You'll need to attract them to the groove of YA literature. To do this, get in tune with what men like: nonfiction, war stories, sex, sports, adventure, and humor all come to mind. Today's YA choices will appeal to male staffers and keep their attention—even the most reluctant.

It won't always be smooth going, but the upside far outweighs the down. Here's an example:

Once upon a time, a young, theatrical, rock-climbing staff member who had worked at our school for many years threw down the gauntlet, "Alison, I'll begin Title Trekking when you begin hiking." This guy, with his unconventional demeanor, seemed to purposefully rub adults the wrong way. I certainly hadn't been able to win him over to the reading program. In fact, I avoided any confrontation of trying to do so. He was a rock-climbing dude, not a bookworm. Yet his student advisee had been a very successful Title Trekker—becoming the eleventh student to read through the entire forty-six titles. Over the summer the maverick advisor teacher and the "reading advisee student" stayed in touch. She encouraged and inspired him.

The following September I was working in the library before our staff meeting. The rock climber strolled in. "Hey Alison," he said, "I read four Title Treks this summer. Here's my journal." He handed it to me. "My advisee is going to begin the program again and I've got to keep up with her," he stated. I was completely taken aback. He took the initiative to participate in a student's program, and he took a risk by sharing his literary comments with me. This nonconforming faculty member gained my whole-hearted admiration and gratitude. Though adults don't always know what to make of him, his students consider him the funkiest teacher in the school. His participation in the reading program encourages students far beyond my wildest and widest scope.

EDUCATING THE EDUCATED

When your word and creative influence aren't swaying the masses, bring in another professional. In the critical effort of having males understand the serious consequence of their influence, we invited Michael Sullivan[3] to help us tackle the boys and books dilemma. We held a special afternoon workshop for our faculty members, and because this problem is not isolated to the school systems, we invited members from the Lake Placid and surrounding communities.

It is amazing how persuasive and revitalizing an outside visiting presenter is for a community of coworkers. There have been so many times that I've been away at conferences and have had the privilege to hear a professional educator who has made a difference in my teaching. Yet I didn't have the background or public speaking talents to most effectively bring the message back to my faculty. That's when I began to approach these professional speakers and inquire whether they might visit a school with a limited budget. I knew such guests would introduce positive and transformative instructional practices in our school.

Having an in-school presentation offers all the pluses of attending a made-to-order workshop with your colleagues, but it leaves the travel woes behind (or to the visitor). It allows coworkers to absorb new information and then apply it in a receptive and collaborative environment. Stimulated from the presentation, staffers brainstorm and bounce new ideas off one another, and then they take them to the classroom.

Most schools have resources for professional development. Bring ideas to your administrator in advance. If you see the opportunity to bring in a professional speaker who will make a difference at your school, do it. Remind your administrator that the cost is much less then sending every faculty member away to separate workshops. Also, if you invite the public, it's great PR, and administrators like that.

SUBTERFUGE, GOOD BOOKS, AND CHOCOLATE

You'll have one chance to hook these doubters, so get it right. Administrators will be mired-down in their cryptic administrative duties and won't have the time. They'll expect that you'll accept their plight and go away. Don't. Keep knocking on their door. Put good novels into their mailboxes. E-mail them gentle, if persistent, nudges, asking how they liked the book. Students love to help get the administration on board. Use your strategic imagination.

Recently I took on a particularly energetic and bright student as a strategic messenger. She was already a committed Title Trekker and just so happened to be taking our headmaster's advanced geometry class. Yes, I admit, the very same headmaster who hadn't yet Title Trekked. Double ouch.

I called my student aside, "How would you like to embark on a secret mission? Independently I've failed. I realize that I need someone with covert skills, a winning personality, and the brilliance to come up with a foolproof weapon unable to be dodged by the slickest guy on the block. Are you up for the task?" She couldn't wait. Another staff member, who had also been unsuccessful in getting the headmaster to Title Trek, was brought into the plan. His response: "Ah yes, the Bulldog—if she can't do it, nobody can." You won't be able to force staff members to participate, but you can engage your manipulative sense of humor and your most persuasive students.

Take stock of your entire audience and assume they will all be a tough sell. Adults are set in their ways, so give them your best pitch. Get out your page-turners. Here's the beauty of it: Young adult titles are that. When you are ready to launch your program, select a wide array of materials, scrutinizing your audience as though you're targeting consumers at a bookstore.

For teachers who lust after outdoor activities, reading young adult titles may feel as though they're veering off the trail. Gary Paulsen has the right stuff. No matter what age group, Paulsen is a winner. His Newbery Award survival adventure, *Hatchet*, remains an excellent choice for reluctant readers. A grown-up's take of Paulsen's *Harris and Me* will discover colorful, laugh-out-loud characters softening a painfully sensitive storyline. His YA autobiographical *How Angel Peterson Got His Name* is a hysterical reminiscence. It will conjure memories for extreme-sport enthusiasts about boyhood life—and near-death—experiences and will ensure a strong staff, and thus student, following. His adult autobiographical *Eastern Sun, Winter Moon* is the perfect choice of a coming-of-age story that men will love. Set in the Philippines during World War II, it's a good selection for war buffs and will surprise readers expecting a cute childhood romp from one of today's most notable YA and children's authors. Adults will shudder at promiscuous adults witnessed through a child's eye. This is NOT a young YA read.

Autobiographies offer up a sound dose of reality, humor, and provide substance for YA skeptics. Jerry Spinelli's *Knots in My Yo-yo String* (NY: Knopf, 1998) is as humorous as it is reflective. Infused with a neighborhood wistfulness recounted from the 1940's and 1950's, you can almost hear Jerry talking, a familiar tone of originality and credibility that is the metaphorical heart of his fiction. From the battered and taped-up hardball of life to a swooning moment in the galaxy of eternity. This slight book will captivate adults with it's simplicity, wit and sense of purpose that distinguishes all of Spinelli's work.

Walter Dean Myers's *Bad Boy* (New York: HarperCollins, 2001) is an autobiographical work that will find a place in many a man's heart. It is a novel that teachers will be able to point students toward who have struggled in a tough environment. It pivots around Myers's early teen years in Harlem. All the teacher support and guidance in the world cannot magically erase the emotional debris from learning disabilities, or from the after-effects of surviving a crack-infested neighborhood. Without educational support, Myers might never have gained confidence to use his writing gifts. This is a book that teachers will connect with—from all angles.

Chris Crutcher's *King of the Mild Frontier* (New York: Greenwillow, 2003) is irresistible. It is at once a laugh-out-loud as well as a wince-with-empathy read. The family dynamics that Crutcher probes will promote interest in reading more of his notable "radical read" YA titles. Crutcher is a master at goading anger, abuse, and emotional discord out of his characters and then offering up personal conquest, survival, and emotional resolutions.

A tech-jolt of creativity emerged in the 2002 season from M.T. Anderson's *Feed* (Cambridge, MA: Candlewick, 2002). It's a title that will appeal to young staff members. The literary draw of *Feed* is to push the envelope, stretch the intellectual senses, and ruffle the moral fabric of our culture. The language, sex, and drug inferences will put sensitive souls on edge and, likewise, will enthrall others. It's the upper school novel on which teachers will itch to get discussion groups going. *Feed* might be used as a companion novel to Nancy Farmer's *The House of the Scorpion* (New York: Atheneum Books for Young Readers, 2002), recipient of the 2003 National Book Award and Printz honor award title.

Fantasy buffs will travel through fresh and complex worlds in Neil Gaiman's subterranean fairyland of *Neverwhere* (New York: Perennial, 2003), and romance seekers will find a blend of new-age mysticism and gothic romance in Liz Berry's *The China Garden* (New York: Farrar, Straus and Giroux, 1996). These titles are entertaining, captivating, and suitable reads for middle school, high school, college, and not-so-young adults.

The following is a sample reading list offering a light blurb about the book. This list is helpful for teachers who want to take a book or two with them over the summer and then select other titles from their hometown public libraries. Give enough information to lead readers toward a book but not so much that the list itself is too wordy to get through. For an expansive list, refer to our Title Trek List, forty-six separate titles that match up with the forty-six high peaks in the Adirondacks. The reading level spans from 3rd grade through high school.

Here's a sample of micro-annotations:

Almond, David. *Skellig*. New York: Delacorte, 1999. What to do with a decrepit angel in your garage? Mystical/allegorical.

Anderson, Laurie Halse. *Catalyst*. New York: Viking, 2002. Ambitious collegiate pursuits versus the necessities of real life.

Berry, Liz. *China Garden*. New York: Farrar, Straus and Giroux, 1996. New-age gothic romance.

Crutcher, Chris. *Ironman*. New York: Greenwillow, 1995. Father/son strife, enduring friendships, and developing triathlon endurance to win emotional battles.

Ellis, Deborah. *The Breadwinner*. Berkeley, CA: Distributed in the USA by Group West, 2001. Courageous girl tip-toeing through travesty, tragedy, and the Taliban.

Gantos, Jack. *Joey Pigza Swallowed the Key*. New York: Farrar, Straus and Giroux, 1998. ADHD/family discord/humor.

Paolini, Christopher. *Eragon*. New York: Random House, 2003. Tapestry of magic, power, elves, dragons, and monsters.

THE END RESULT

Broadcasting the incredible books out there for your whole school will change the intellectual climate of your school. Having adults come looking for more good books in the school library casts radiant approval upon the collection. When adults are spending time browsing in the library, impromptu conversations will stimulate collaboration in multiple ways: how to use a novel in a class or book club, or shared excitement about how a book is *perfect* for a particular student. Students have access to these books, but they need adults to call their attention to them.

Six years after our young adult reading program for adults began, the response remains overwhelming. Adults love the stuff. What started as a reading initiative idea to get adults up to speed on YA books has become an ingrained part of our program. Teachers are reading children's and YA titles like crazy. Four faculty members have become Literary 46'ers, having read and journaled every title on the reading lists. Two began another go-around. Title Trekking is not just for students. It's a whole-school trend.

Like the phenomenon of exercise and a healthy diet, the more exposure and familiarity your staff have, the more trained and comfortable they'll become. Most important, the more likely they'll popularize these books throughout the student population. As your staff is visibly reading and enjoying these books, the community interest in the material grows. Teen literature in the hands (and hearts) of the educators who work with teens is a no-brainer.

Adult interest in children's and YA titles has its own healthy following at North Country School. The program's momentum comes from personal communication and encouragement: staff sharing good books with their students, staff sharing books with each another, and students sharing books with their teachers. When adults and students are openly receptive, responsive, and connected about the books that they're reading, a communication gap is bridged and literature has a place within the community.

NOTES

1. Michael Sullivan, *Connecting Boys with Books, What Libraries Can Do* (Chicago: American Library Association, 2003), p. 1.

2. Ibid., p. 9.

3. Michael Sullivan, speaker, presenter, author.

CONCLUSION
It Makes a Difference

Literature is an ingrained part of my life. It sheltered me from a mean reality and offered positive stories of achievement. Literature enabled me to beat the verbal and psychological abuse that I absorbed while growing up. Reading was not an escape—it was sustenance, opportunity, and alternative; stability within an out-of-whack reality.

Even when I was young, I knew my older sister was very smart. She read. She read a lot. I equated reading with intelligence. My grandmother, anxious to intervene in our little-family disaster, did what she could. She loaded our bookshelves with titles such as: *The Call of the Wild*, *Alice in Wonderland*, *The Arabian Nights*, *Swiss Family Robinson*, *The Five Little Peppers & How They Grew*, *Peter Pan*, and on and on. They were books too old for my five-year-old abilities, but I admired my sister and wanted to be like her. So I began to read what she was reading. Books didn't miraculously make me smart; in fact, many times I didn't have a clue what the stories were about. But I emulated my sister and kept at it. I believed that if I read enough I could be her.

What reading did do was enlarge my world and vocabulary. While I suffered dreadfully in social and academic environments, my reading comprehension soared. I powered through the concrete and reveled in abstract concepts. Quietly, I tiptoed through stories that propelled me beyond adult ridicule, judgment, and extrinsically imposed limits. When my best friend came over and my stepfather began humiliating me, she and I would dash off giggling in nervous embarrassment. In my room we would squirrel ourselves away and read together for hours.

A therapist once asked me about growing up. "Was anyone paying attention to you?" It was a good question, under the circumstances it was better when they weren't. I spent endless hours reading without interruption. It was great. Reading was my glass half-full.

So it is natural that I want children in a world fraught with crisis, disappointments, manipulative marketing, political brainwashing, and fraying family ties to have an option of hope, resolution, and choice. Reading is freedom.

I truly believe that being able to read for enjoyment is an essential component to the emotional well-being and intellectual empowerment of our children. In this book, you've learned of programming that celebrates the reader in the corner as well as strives to popularize the communal act of enjoying a good book.

A 2003 survey conducted by the National Center for Education Statistics was released in December 2005. It determined that literacy among the higher educated in our country has dropped significantly. Of adults who have taken graduate courses, or have graduate degrees, only 41 percent scored as proficient in their reading skills—a 10 percent drop from the survey taken ten years ago. This study was not designed to assess whether people can read a novel, but whether their competency level enabled them to read a map or directions for taking medication.[1]

"When the test was last administered, in 1992, 40 percent of the nation's college graduates scored at the proficient level, meaning that they were able to read lengthy, complex English texts and draw complicated inferences. But on the 2003 test, only 31 percent of the graduates demonstrated those high-level skills. There were 26.4 million college graduates."[2]

Colleges blame middle and secondary education. Schools blame home use of computers and idle hours spent in front of the television. Parents blame schools. Everyone seems befuddled. Many colleges offer remedial reading classes for entering freshman, suggesting that high school graduates really aren't prepared for the literacy requirements of higher education. And despite higher education, adult literacy dropped or was flat across every level of education, from people with graduate degrees to those who dropped out of high school.

Grover J. Whitehurst, director of the institute within the Department of Education that helped to oversee the test, believes that the literacy of college graduates had dropped because a rising number of young Americans in recent years had spent their free time watching television and surfing the Internet. "We're seeing substantial declines in reading for pleasure, and it's showing up in our literacy levels," Whitehurst said.[3]

Clearly, if we want literacy rates to rise, we need to change our educational tactics. This book has given you several suggestions on practices to tweak and programming to implement. A school year is shorter than a regular year, by a good two months; it's about nine months for most of us, figuring in holidays and vacations. Assuming that you're in a school with other creative educators, every department's program cannot be fit in, fully attended, or have engaged participation all of the time. Within the too-short school year are science fairs, art fairs, theatrical presentations, guest artists, musical performances, sports events, holiday festivities, field trips, class trips, CAT tests, ERB, SSAT, SAT testing, snow days, and the "normal" academic day. Every required and special program is running pell-mell over the other. Not only that, but take a glance at the list of after-school activities tacked on any family's refrigerator. Who has time to read?

Look at the overall picture and take your time. Don't exacerbate the situation by not pacing yourself. Don't get caught up in the hubbub.

The programs that I have presented work because they get kids reading. None of them came about all at once. They developed slowly with much trial and error along the way. Each program stands alone, but all of them woven together fortify the entire educational experience like individual strengths build a community. These programs build upon one another and become stronger each year.

Am I there yet? Not even close. I'm lobbying for more silent reading time during the academic day, for more read-aloud time for all grades, and for graphic novels and comic books to litter the classroom and family room. That's for starters. Here's the thing: As intelligent adults we can make a difference.

Life is moving very quickly. Take your cue, and slowly and carefully implement a program that you feel strongly about. Plan it, care about it, develop it, and be proud of the quality and the outcome of your best efforts. Encouraging children to take time to read good books; to slow their frenetic pace in a stressful time; to become empowered to read, choose, judge, and think for themselves—all of this is a right. It's our right to help get them to exercise it.

The fact is that reading does enrich cognitive thinking skills. By middle and high school, the librarian's daily responsibilities increase dramatically to focus on research instruction and there is a negligent decrease in sharing literature with upper school students. If educators are serious about encouraging students to read, they must provide time and instruction, as well as include knowledgeable and experienced librarians in the process. By implementing practical and logical programming into a student's secondary education, we'll help shift plummeting literacy statistics. Across the country people are reading in groups. Adults enjoy the social aspects of reading *together*. Women, men, friends, Oprah—book clubs are in! What part of this is so difficult for educators to understand?

Schools are full of community potential—classrooms, activity groups, special arts blocks—there are any number of natural breakout sections. Within this ready-made system, librarians have what it takes to give students a leg-up to literacy success.

Let's help students out of the limitations of the system by leading from within. I hope this book has motivated you to begin a literature movement in your school.

NOTES

1. Liz Bowie, "Better Educated but Less Literate, Degree Not Always Guarantee of Skills," *Sun Reporter*, Dec. 16, 2005.

2. Sam Dillon, "Literacy Falls For Graduates From College, Testing Finds," *New York Times*, Dec. 16, 2005, p. A34 (L).

3. Ibid.

BIBLIOGRAPHY

Almond, David. *Skellig*. New York: Delacorte, 1999.

Al-Windawi, Thura. *Thura's Diary: My Life in Wartime Iraq*. New York: Viking, 2004.

Anderson, Laurie Halse. *Catalyst*. New York: Viking, 2002.

———. *Speak*. New York: Farrar, Straus and Giroux, 1999.

Anderson, M.T. *Feed*. Cambridge, MA: Candlewick, 2002.

Anonymous. *Go Ask Alice*. Englewood Cliffs, NJ: Prentice-Hall, 1971.

Appelt, Kathi. *Kissing Tennessee: And Other Stories from the Stardust Dance*. New York: Harcourt, 2000.

———. *My Father's Summers, A Daughter's Memoir*. New York: Holt, 2004.

Armstrong, Lance, and Sally Jenkins. *It's Not about the Bike: My Journey Back to Life*. New York: Berkley, 2001.

Baker, Jeannie. *Window*. New York: Greenwillow, 1991.

Barrett, Peter. *To Break the Silence: Thirteen Short Stories for Young Readers*. New York: Dell, 1986.

Bartel, Julie. "The Good, the Bad, and the Edgy." *School Library Journal*. July 2005, Vol. 51, Iss. 7, pp. 33–41.

Baxter, Kathleen. *Gotcha Again: More Nonfiction Booktalks*. Westport, CT: Libraries Unlimited, 2002.

Berry, Liz. *The China Garden*. New York: Farrar, Straus and Giroux, 1996.

Birkerts, Sven. "The Truth about Reading." *School Library Journal*. Nov. 2004, Vol. 50, Iss. 11, pp. 50–52.

Bloor, Edward. *Tangerine*. San Diego, CA: Harcourt Brace, 1997.

Bradbury, Ray. *Fahrenheit 451*. New York: Ballantine, 1953.

Bradman, Tony, ed. *Skin Deep*. UK: Puffin, 2004.

Brashares, Ann. *The Sisterhood of the Traveling Pants*. New York: Delacorte, 2001.

Bridges, Ruby. *Through My Eyes*. New York: Scholastic, 1999.

Bruchac, James. *How the Chipmunk Got His Stripes*. New York: Dial, 2001.

———. *Native American Games & Stories*. Golden, CO: Fulcrum, 2001.

———. *Skeleton Man*. New York: HarperCollins, 2001.

Bruchac, James, and Joseph Bruchac. *When the Chenoo Howls*. New York: Walker, 1998.

Bruchac, Joseph, and Sally Wern Comport. *The Dark Pond*. New York: HarperCollins, 2004.

Burgess, Melvin. *Smack*. New York: Henry Holt, 1998.

Buss, Fran Leeper. *Journey of the Sparrows*. New York: Dell, 1991.

Carver, Peter. *Close Ups: Best Stories for Teens*. Red Deer, AL: Red Deer, 2000.

Cary, Lorene. *Black Ice*. New York: Random House, 1991.

Chbosky, Stephen. *The Perks of Being a Wallflower*. New York: Pocket, 1999.

Cleary, Beverly. *Dear Mr. Henshaw*. New York: Scholastic, 1983.

Cormier, Robert. *Frenchtown Summer*. New York: Delacorte, 1999.

Creech, Sharon. *Granny Torrelli Makes Soup*. New York: Scholastic, 2003.

——. *Heartbeat*. New York: HarperCollins, 2004.

——. *Love That Dog*. New York: Harper Trophy, 2001.

——. *Walk Two Moons*. New York: Scholastic, 1994.

Crew, Linda. *Children of the River*. New York: Delacorte, 1989.

Crist-Evans, Craig. *North of Everything*. Cambridge, MA: Candlewick, 2004.

Crutcher, Chris. *Athletic Shorts*. New York: Greenwillow, 1991.

——. *Chinese Handcuffs*. New York: Greenwillow, 1989.

——. *The Crazy Horse Electric Game*. New York: Greenwillow, 1987.

——. *Ironman: A Novel*. New York: Greenwillow, 1995.

——. *King of the Mild Frontier: An Ill-Advised Autobiography*. New York: Greenwillow, 2003.

——. *The Sledding Hill*. New York: Greenwillow, 2005.

——. *Stotan*. New York: Greenwillow, 1986.

——. *Whale Talk*. New York: Greenwillow, 2001.

Cushman, Karen. *Catherine, Called Birdy*. New York: Clarion, 1994.

Dahl, Roald. *The BFG*. New York: Farrar, Straus and Giroux, 1982.

——. *Charlie and the Chocolate Factory*. New York: Puffin, 1973.

Danziger, Paula, and Ann M. Martin. *P.S. Longer Letter Later*. New York: Scholastic, 1998.

Darby, Mary Ann, and Miki Pryne. *Hearing All the Voices*. Lanham, MD: Scarecrow, 2002.

DiCamillo, Kate. *Because of Winn-Dixie*. Cambridge, MA: Candlewick, 2000.

Donnelly, Jennifer. Closing speech at the New York Library Association's Youth Services Section *Bringing the Pieces Together* spring conference, April 1, 2005, Bolton Landing, NY.

——. *A Northern Light*. San Diego, CA: Harcourt, 2003.

Duder, Tessa. *In Lane Three, Alex Archer*. Boston: Houghton Mifflin, 1989.

Elledge, Scott. *Wider Than the Sky: Poems to Grow Up With*. New York: HarperCollins, 1990.

Ellis, Deborah. *The Breadwinner*. Berkeley, CA: Group West, 2001.

Eye Spy. Chicago: World Book, 1996.

Farmer, Nancy. *The Ear, the Eye, and the Arm*. Waterville, ME: Thorndike, 2005.

——. *The House of the Scorpion*. New York: Atheneum Books for Young Readers, 2002.

Flagg, Fannie. *Daisy Fay and the Miracle Man*. New York: Warner, 1992.

Fleischman, John. *Phineas Gage: A Gruesome but True Story about Brain Science*. New York: Houghton Mifflin, 2002.

Fleischman, Sid. *The Abracadabra Kid a Writer's Life*. New York: Greenwillow, 1996.

Fleischman, Sid, and Peter Sís. *The Whipping Boy*. New York: Greenwillow, 1986.

Fletcher, Ralph. *Marshfield Dreams*. New York: Henry Holt, 2005.

Forian, Douglas. *Omnibeasts*. Orlando, FL: Harcourt, 2004.

Frost, Helen. *Keesha's House*. New York: Farrar, Straus and Giroux, 2003.

Gaiman, Neil. *Coraline*. New York: Harper Trophy, 2004.

——. *Neverwhere*. New York: Perennial, 2003.

Gallo, Donald, ed. *Destination Unexpected*. Cambridge, MA: Candlewick, 2003.

——. *First Crossing: Stories about Teen Immigrants*. Cambridge, MA: Candlewick, 2004.

——. *Join in Multiethnic Short Stories*. New York: Delacorte, 1993.

——. *No Easy Answers: Short Stories about Teens Making Tough Choices*. New York: Delacorte, 1997.

——. *Speaking for Ourselves*. Urbana, IL: NCTE, 1990.

Gantos, Jack. *Heads or Tails: Stories from the 6th Grade*. New York: Farrar, Straus and Giroux, 1994.

——. *Hole in My Life*. New York: Farrar, Straus and Giroux, 2002.

———. *Jack Adrift: Fourth Grade without a Clue*. New York: Farrar, Straus and Giroux, 2003.

———. *Jack on the Tracks: Four Seasons of Fifth Grade*. New York: Farrar, Straus and Giroux, 1999.

———. *Jack's Black Book*. New York: Farrar, Straus and Giroux, 1997.

———. *Jack's New Power: Stories from a Caribbean Year*. New York: Farrar, Straus and Giroux, 1995.

———. *Joey Pigza Swallowed the Key*. New York: Farrar, Straus and Giroux, 1998.

George, Jean Craighead, and John Schoenherr. *Julie of the Wolves*. New York: Harper & Row, 1972.

Giff, Patricia Reilly. *Don't Tell the Girls*. New York: Holiday House, 2005.

Gioa, Dana. "Reading at Risk: A Survey of Literary Reading in America," Research Division Report #46, National Endowment for the Arts, 2002.

Golding, William. *Lord of the Flies*. New York: Coward-McCann, 1954.

Gordon, Sheila. *Waiting for the Rain: A Novel of South Africa*. New York: Bantam, 1989.

Greenberg, Jan. *Heart to Heart: New Poems Inspired by Twentieth-Century American Art*. New York: Abrams, 2001.

Grimes, Nikki. *Bronx Masquerade*. New York: Dial, 2002.

———. *Tai Chi Morning: Snapshots of China*. Chicago: Cricket, 2004.

Haddon, Mark. *The Curious Incident of the Dog in the Night-time*. New York: Doubleday, 2003.

Hamill, Pete. *Snow in August: A novel*. Boston: Little, Brown, 1997.

Handford, Martin. *Where's Waldo?* Cambridge, MA: Candlewick, 1997.

Hemingway, Ernest. *The Nick Adams Stories*. New York: Scribner, 1981.

Hesse, Karen. *Letters from Rifka*. New York: Henry Holt, 1992.

———. *Out of the Dust*. New York: Scholastic, 1997.

Humphrey, Jack. "There Is No Simple Way to Build a Middle School Reading Program." *Phi Delta Kappan*, June 2002, Vol. 83, Iss. 10, p. 754.

Hurston, Zora Neale. *Dust Tracks on a Road*. New York: HarperTrade, 1996.

———. *The Skull Talks Back*, adapted by Joyce Carol Thomas. New York: HarperCollins, 2004.

Johnson, Angela. *The First Part Last*. New York: Simon & Schuster Books for Young Readers, 2003.

———. *Gone from Home*. New York: DK Ink/Richard Jackson, 1998.

Katz, Susan. *A Revolutionary Field Trip*. New York: Simon & Schuster, 2004.

Kidd, Sue Monk. *The Secret Life of Bees*. New York: Viking, 2002.

Kimmel, Haven. *A Girl Named Zippy Growing Up Small in Mooreland, Indiana*. New York: Doubleday, 2001.

Klause, Annette Curtis. *The Silver Kiss*. New York: Delacorte, 1990.

Kobrin, Beverly. *Eyeopeners II: Children's Books to Answer Children's Questions about the World Around Them*. New York: Scholastic, 1995.

Krashen, Stephen. *The Power of Reading*. Westport, CT: Libraries Unlimited, 2004.

———. "What Do We Know about Libraries and Reading Achievement?" *Book Report*, Jan./Feb. 2002, Vol. 20, Iss. 4, p. 38.

Lear, Edward. *Complete Nonsense Book*. New York: Dodd, Mead, 1962, c1912.

Lee, Harper. *To Kill a Mockingbird*. London: Heinemann, 1960.

Levithan, David. *Realm of Possibilities*. New York: Knopf, 2004.

———. *Where We Are, What We See*. New York: Scholastic/Push Cart, 2005.

Lipsyte, Robert. *The Contender*. New York: Harper & Row, 1967.

Mackler, Carolyn. *The Earth, My Butt, and Other Big, Round Things*. Cambridge, MA: Candlewick, 2003.

Magic Eye 3D Illusions. Kansas City, MO: Andrews and McMeel, 1996.

Mankell, Henning. *Secrets in the Fire*. Toronto: Annick, 2003.

Mathew, L.S. *Fish*. New York: Delacorte, 2004.

McDonald, Janet. *Brother Hood*. New York: Farrar, Straus and Giroux, 2004.

———. *Chill Wind*. New York: Farrar, Straus and Giroux, 2002.

———. *Project Girl*. New York: Farrar, Straus and Giroux, 1999.

———. *Spellbound*. New York: Frances Foster, 2001.

———. *Twists and Turns*. New York: Frances Foster, 2003.

McKibbon, Bill. *Wandering Home*. New York: Crown, 2005.

McWhirter, Ross, and Norris McWhirter. *Guinness Book of World Records*. London: Guilane Entertainment, 2003.

Meltzer, Milton. *Langston Hughes: An Illustrated Edition*. Brookfield, CT: Millbrook, 1997.

Merrill, Billy. *Talking in the Dark*. New York: Scholastic/Push Cart, 2003.

Moeyaert, Bart. *Brothers*. Asheville, NC: Front Street, 2005.

Mosher, Howard Frank. *Northern Borders*. New York: Doubleday, 1994.

Mosher, Richard. *Zazoo*. New York: Clarion, 2001.

Myers, Walter Dean. *Bad Boy*. New York: HarperCollins, 2001.

———. *Blues Journey*. New York: Holiday House, 2003.

———. *Here in Harlem: Poems in Many Voices*. New York: Holiday House, 2004.

Nelson, Marilyn. *Carver: A Life in Poems*. Asheville, NC: Front Street, 2001.

———. *Fortune's Bones: The Manumission Requiem*. Asheville, NC: Front Street, 2004.

Nye, Naomi Shahib. *I Feel a Little Jumpy Around You*. New York: Simon & Schuster, 1996.

———. *19 Varieties of Gazelle*. New York: Greenwillow, 2002.

O'Brien, Robert C., and Zena Bernstein. *Mrs. Frisby and the Rats of Nimh*. New York: Atheneum, 1971.

Olshan, Joseph. *Clara's Heart: A Novel*. New York: Arbor House, 1985.

Orwell, George. *Animal Farm*. New York: Harcourt, Brace, 1954.

Panzer, Nora. *Celebrate America: In Poetry and Art*. New York: Hyperion, 1994.

Paolini, Christopher. *Eldest*. New York: Random House, 2005.

———. *Eragon*. New York: Random House, 2003.

Park, Barbara. *Mick Harte Was Here*. New York: Alfred A. Knopf, 1995.

Park, Linda Sue. *A Single Shard*. New York: Clarion, 2001.

Paterson, Katherine, and Donna Diamond. *Bridge to Terabithia*. New York: Crowell, 1977.

Paulsen, Gary. *Eastern Sun, Winter Moon*. New York: Harcourt Brace, 1993.

———. *How Angel Peterson Got His Name*. New York: Wendy Lamb, 2003.

Plath, Sylvia. *The Bell Jar*. New York: Harper & Row, 1971.

Plum-Ucci, Carol. *The Body of Christopher Creed*. New York: Volo/Hyperion, 2001.

Pullman, Philip. *The Amber Spyglass*. New York: Alfred A. Knopf, 2000.

———. *The Golden Compass*. New York: Alfred A. Knopf, 1996.

———. *The Subtle Knife*. New York: Distributed by Random House, 1997.

Rochman, Hazel. *Against Borders*. Chicago: American Library Association, 1993.

Rochman, Hazel, and Darleen McCampbell. *Leaving Home: Stories*. New York: Harper-Collins, 1998.

Rohmann, Eric. *Time Flies*. New York: Crown, 1994.

Riordan, Rick. *The Lightening Thief*. New York: Hyperion, 2005.

Sachar, Louis. *Holes*. New York: Scholastic, 1989.

Salinger, J.D. *The Catcher in the Rye*. Boston: Little, Brown, 1951.

———. *Nine Stories*. New York: Bantam, 1964.

Salisbury, Graham. *Island Boyz*. New York: Wendy Lamb, 2002.

Schmidt, Gary. *Lizzie Bright and the Buckminster Boy*. New York: Clarion, 2004.

Scieszka, Jon. *Guys Write for Guys Read*. New York: Viking, 2005.

Scieszka, Jon, and Lane Smith. *Science Verse*. New York: Viking, 2004.

Seidler, Tor, and Jon Agee. *Mean Margaret*. New York: HarperCollins, 1997.

Silverstein, Shel. *Falling Up*. New York: Harper & Collins, 1996.

———. *Where the Sidewalk Ends*. New York: Harper & Row, 1974.

Singer, Marilyn. *Central Heating: Poems about Fire and Heating*. New York: Alfred A. Knopf, 2005.

———. *Make Me Over*. New York: Dutton Children's, 2005.

Smith, Jessie Carney, and Joseph M. Palmisano, eds. *Reference Library of Black America*. [Farmington Hills, MI: African American Publications, Proteus Enterprises, Gale Group, 2000.

Solheim, James. *It's Disgusting and I Ate It!* New York: Simon & Schuster, 1998.

Spinelli, Jerry. *Crash*. New York: Random House, 1996.

———. *Loser*. New York: Joanna Cotler, 2002.

———. *Maniac Magee: A Novel*. Boston: Little, Brown, 1990.

———. *Stargirl*. New York: Random House, 2000.

———. *Knots in My Yo-yo*. New York: Knopf, 1998.

Staples, Suzanne Fisher. *Dangerous Skies*. New York: Farrar, Straus and Giroux, 1996.

———. *Shabanu: Daughter of the Wind*. New York: Alfred A. Knopf, 1991.

Stern, Jerome, ed. *Micro Fiction: An Anthology of Really Short Stories*. New York: W.W. Norton, 1996.

Stevenson, Robert Louis. *A Child's Garden of Verses*. New York: Golden, c1978.

Stratton, Allan. *Chanda's Secret*. New York: Annick, 2004.

Sullivan, Ed. "Fiction or Poetry?" *School Library Journal*, Aug. 2003, Vol. 49, Iss. 8, p. 44.

Sullivan, Michael. *Connecting Boys to Books*. Chicago: American Library Association, 2003.

———. "Why Johny Won't Read: Schools Often Dismiss What Boys Like. No Wonder They're Not Wild About Reading." *School Library Journal*, Aug. 2004, Vol. 50, Iss. 8, pp. 36–39.

Taylor, Mildred D. *Roll of Thunder, Hear My Cry*. New York: Dial, 1976.

Trelease, Jim. *The Read-Aloud Handbook*. New York: Penguin, 2001.

Van Allsburg, Chris. *The Mysteries of Harris Burdick*. Boston: Houghton Mifflin, 1984.

Watkins, Yoko Kawashima. *So Far from the Bamboo Grove*. New York: Lothrop, Lee & Shepard, 1986.

Weil, Sylvia. *My Guardian Angel*. New York: A.A. Levine, 2004.

Wick, Walter, and Jean Marzollo. *I Spy Super Challenger! A Book of Picture Riddles*. New York: Scholastic, 1997.

Wolff, Virginia Euwer. *Make Lemonade*. New York: Henry Holt, 1993.

Woodson, Jacqueline. *Locomotion*. New York: G.P. Putnam's Sons, 2003.

Wynne-Jones, Tim. *The Boy in the Burning House*. New York: Farrar, Straus and Giroux, 2001.

———. *Some of the Kinder Planets*. New York: Orchard, 1995.

———. *A Thief in the House of Memory*. New York: Farrar, Straus and Giroux, 2005.

Young, Cathy. *One Hot Second: Stories about Desire*. New York: Knopf Books for Young Readers, 2002.

Zindel, Paul. *The Pigman and Me*. New York: Bantam, 1991.

INDEX

ABOUT THE AUTHOR

ALISON M. G. FOLLOS has been the librarian at North Country School in Lake Placid, NY, since 1989. She has worked as the private librarian for an entrepreneur and written feature articles for regional and national publications. She is a contributing book reviewer for *School Library Journal* and has published numerous articles on school library programming. Alison has served on her town's public library board, the Lake Placid School Board, and the Franklin-Essex-Hamilton School Library Systems Council of New York. She is a member of American Library Association, Association for Library Services to Children, and the New York Library Association. She lives on the AuSable River in the Adirondack Mountains of New York with her husband and their dog.